Jam for Tea

Cathy Murray

When my mother-in-law, Rose Murray, was ninety two years old she started to write about her life but it was too late. She couldn't sustain the interest or the concentration. All she managed to capture was a short memoir about her childhood. We regretted not helping Rose to record her life story but the experience proved the inspiration for my own writing.

My childhood memories are from the 1950s and I recalled them for my book "Cabbage and Semolina". Lots of readers told me they'd enjoyed "Cabbage and Semolina" so I'm pleased to offer some more reminiscences and anecdotes from both the 1950s and the 1960s which I hope you enjoy.

JAM FOR TEA

Contents

WILLING SHILLING

One thing leads to another and one person's reminiscence starts someone else on their "do you remember?" journey. After reading "Cabbage and Semolina", my younger sister got talking to me on the phone one afternoon about the Brownies. "Do you remember," she asked, "how each week we waited by ourselves to catch the bus into Wakefield to go to Brownies? And how if there was enough time we'd walk and save the fare money for sweets? And what about that boxer dog that stood near the bus stop and snarled at us?"

After I told her I remembered the dog vividly my sister added, "And do you remember Willing Shilling?"

"Willing Shilling? Whatever was that?"

"Well, it was like the Bob-a-Job the Boy Scouts did; only this was for the girls."

And then I did remember. Yes, Willing Shilling. The annual Girl Guides and Brownies fund-raising week when we did chores for our mum, grandma, aunts and other relatives who paid us a shilling for every job. Dusting the furniture; wiping the downstairs windows; sparkling the brasses; and industrial scale shoe polishing. At home washing-up, drying-up and putting-away weren't included in Willing Shilling because we had to do those tasks anyway. By the end of the week we'd earned several shillings. And twenty jobs raised one whole pound for Brownie funds!

At the next Brownie meeting we proudly handed the cash to our leader, Brown Owl, who in return, signed off our Willing Shilling collecting cards. What the Willing Shilling money was spent on I don't know. But, plus our weekly subs, it must have been enough to keep the Brownie pack going because we didn't do Willing Shilling again until the following year.

However, each year we were also asked to sell "Sunny Smiles". The sunny smiles were photographs of small children. The photos were black and white, about two inches square and perforated into a little booklet. We had to ask our family and friends to buy the photos to raise money for disadvantaged children. The prospective purchaser had to choose, tear out and keep the photo of the child they wished to buy. We felt sorry for the children and extra sorry for those who weren't picked. In the end our mum bought all the children in the booklet who were left behind.

I joined the Brownies when I was about eight years old and was allocated to the Fairies. There were Fairies, Elves, Kelpies and Pixies: four "sixes" for the twenty four girls in our Brownie pack. There was a waiting list for places and the limit was never exceeded. A newcomer had to wait for a girl to become old enough to leave the Brownies and join the Girl Guides thus creating a place for the next younger girl in the queue.

The oldest girl in each "six" was the leader and called "The Sixer". The next oldest was the second-in-command and known as "The Seconder". If you knew the birthdays of the other girls it was easy to work out when it would be your turn to be promoted and take charge of a six. I couldn't wait; I yearned to be a Sixer.

Meanwhile, we collected badges such as the Hostess badge; the Bird Watcher's badge; the Book Lover's badge; the Musician badge. In order to gain a badge several tasks had to be undertaken. Every few weeks part of the Brownie meeting was spent deciding which badge to work for next. Once confident the criteria for attaining the badge had been met, Brown Owl would arrange for us to be assessed by a tester. Our mum was the tester for the Book Lover's badge because she'd been a library assistant before she was married. She occasionally came to Brownie meetings to test other girls on their knowledge of the books they'd read so they could gain the badge. Mum wasn't allowed to test my sister and me because that wouldn't have been fair so, for the Book Lover's badge, we were tested by Brown Owl.

For the Hostess badge, four girls at a time would go to the home of an elderly lady in a posh part of Wakefield to serve tea using her best bone china plates, cups and saucers. The stress of not dropping the china was so great it caused a tuneful rattling sound as the tea was served. Afterwards, the pots were washed-up and left dry and sparkling (and hopefully chip-free) on the sideboard.

I gained the Musician badge by asking my piano teacher, Miss Heaps, to certify that I could fulfil all the requirements set out in the Brownie Handbook. That was an easy badge to obtain as it was like a piano exam and by then I'd passed Grade Two. Unlike the Bird Watcher's badge which was far from easy. Despite the many lumps of stale bread I strewed all over our garden, I never spotted anything other than a few sparrows and a chirpy robin. My dad put an end to my bird watching ambitions when he decided I was more likely to gain the Rat Watcher's badge and banned any further bread scattering!

Apart from planning for the next badge, the weekly Brownie meeting was spent learning useful things like how to tie knots and bandage a broken finger. We played games of the chasing variety and when we were exhausted quieter ones such as "Kim's Game" and "I-Spy". We took turns to prepare the refreshments (usually orange squash and biscuits) which were served half way through the meeting.

There was the ritual of the weekly opening and closing ceremony. At the beginning of each meeting all the girls and the leaders stood in a circle around a large papier maché toadstool. We sang songs, said prayers and answered, "Yes, Brown Owl", in roll-call. Occasionally, there was the enrolment ceremony for a new recruit. The initiate simultaneously placed two fingers on the toadstool and recited a solemn promise while making the special Brownie salute. This was two-fingered but with the 'V' closed and the arm bent at the elbow so the salute was vertical and at shoulder height.

Once initiated into the Brownies we were supposed to do a good turn for someone every day. And we always had to "Be Prepared" which meant never going outdoors without a whistle and some string. To this day I always carry a ball of string in the car. Very useful it is too. On one occasion our exhaust fell down and scraped along the ground as we were leaving a car park. I astonished my husband by leaping out and square lashing the exhaust firmly back into position where it remained until we arrived at the repair centre fifteen miles away!

Brownie uniform was... well... all brown. We wore knee-length, long-sleeved tunics with a leather belt around the middle and also a Brownie hat and necktie. On enrolment we were awarded a special shiny Brownie badge to pin on our ties. As each new badge was acquired it was sewn onto the tunic sleeve. There was a special badge to sew above the tunic pocket denoting the six to which each girl belonged. The Seconder had one gold stripe on her sleeve and the Sixer had two gold stripes. Shoe style was not specified except they had to be brown or black and sensible.

At the end of the meeting we stood in the circle again, said a prayer and sang "Brownie Bells".

Oh Lord, our God,
Thy children call,
Grant us thy peace,

Til the sunrise.
Good Night.
This was sung to the tune used for Big Ben, church bells and ice-cream vans. After the song we wished each other goodbye until the next meeting.

I loved going to Brownies. It was so organised and well structured. The games and company of other children were great fun. But it was the useful things we learned that I really enjoyed and the anticipation of taking charge of a Six. The night I was appointed the Sixer of The Kelpies was one of the high spots of my life thus far.

On special occasions there were Brownie parties which sometimes included fancy dress costumes. Our mother was good at sewing and making clothes and when she discovered that she could sew crepe paper with her Singer Sewing Machine her creative talents went to a whole new level. For me she made a multi-layered "Little Bo-Peep" dress from white crepe paper arranged over her own pale blue satin petticoat temporarily shortened for the occasion. The dress had a big, pink crepe paper bow around the middle. She made a shepherd's crook from a broom handle to which she attached a curved cardboard top and tied another big pink crepe paper bow beneath. For my younger sister our mum went all artistic and designed a crepe paper dress in various shades of green to which she glued pictures from bulb catalogues. "What are you supposed to be?" several Brownies asked my younger sister. "Spring, of course," she replied stiffly. There wasn't much room for manoeuvre in a crepe paper dress!

By the end of the evening, after the usual jostling and chasing games, our dresses were in shreds but fortunately we had some spare clothes with us. "Be Prepared" wasn't just the Brownies motto: it was one of our mother's favourite maxims too.

When it was time to leave the Brownies I went straight into the Girl Guides. However, my younger sister quit and took up pony riding in return for cleaning out the owner's stables. Willing Shilling came round each year and my search for the jobs extended to our neighbours and, eventually, all the houses along the street. This consequently increased the amount of money raised. As I got older the jobs got bigger and included shopping, leaf sweeping, ironing and baby-minding. These usually earned a donation of two and six (two shillings and sixpence) and once I even got ten bob (ten shillings). But for a full clean and polish of a large red and white Austin Cambridge I thought a donation of just one shilling was a bit mean. Willing Shilling! One of Girl Guiding's many lessons for life.

Apart from our weekly pocket money, birthday money and Christmas money we didn't have much disposable cash. The point of pocket money was to help you learn that money was earned and didn't grow on trees. Keep your bedroom tidy; make your bed each morning; help with the washing-up. The pocket money was measured out in pennies and increased annually not because of inflation but because we'd become one year older. I didn't properly appreciate that pocket money was our reward for doing chores because whether the bedroom was tidy or not, the bedclothes left in a heap and the pots left on the draining board, the pocket money still continued to be paid out to my sister and me every Saturday morning. That was typical of our mum. She was one of the kindest people I've ever known.

Every year a "gentleman of the road" would call at our house and request some water. My mum always gave him some cheese sandwiches and a cup of tea. She put a chair for him outside the back door and he'd sit there for a few minutes enjoying the refreshments. The tramp said very few words and when he'd finished his snack my mum would offer him any clothes our dad didn't want any more. The man would pick out what he wanted, mumble a few words of what I presumed were thanks and be on his way. It was the same person every year and how my mum came to know him is unclear. When we asked why she looked after him she just said she felt sorry for him and that was that.

Every week the pocket money went straight into our money boxes which were a Christmas present staple from distant aunties. One year my sister and I each received a replica Posting Box made of tin into which you posted coins and could only open the base to retrieve them with the aid of a nail file. Another time we got a china pig with a slot in its back and no apparent means of opening it except with a hammer. And once we were given a proper, locking cash box made from black lacquered tin with gold decorative lines and a real key. Unfortunately, the same key fitted both cash boxes and my sister was persistently perplexed as to why her pile of pennies never seemed to increase as much as mine even when the age-weighted pocket money differential was taken into account.

We saved up so we would have some spending money when we went on our annual holiday to the seaside. Being a public health officer, our dad didn't approve of candyfloss or toffee apples which he regarded as unhygienic; but being a pragmatist he knew we would learn

11

best from our mistakes. So, candyfloss and toffee apples were on the list of "if you want it you'll have to pay for it yourself." And so were the slot machines. Put a penny in the top; watch the silver ball appear; flick the ball into a winning hole and see the prize pennies tumbling into the drawer at the bottom. Except they usually didn't and there was nothing for it but to try again. And again. And again. Until the money ran out and a year's worth of carefully harboured pennies was gone.

At Junior school, being a bookish child, I was asked by the teacher to take charge of the class library. This was a crate of books which were given out once a week at "library time". The books were looked at or read for half an hour and then packed away in the box until the following week. Each child kept the same book every week and was only allowed to change it on "swapping day". My job was to hand out the books and collect them in again at the end of library time. I had to check that each child's name card was inserted between the pages of the book. This was to ensure that a check for any scribbles or finger-marks left in the book could be attributed to the correct culprit on swapping day.

A couple of times each term the class was taken for a swap session to the central store of books locked in two cupboards in the corridor outside the Headmaster's office. If the previously selected book was still being read and enjoyed, that was too bad. You still had to swap it so that everyone had a turn with the best books available. No hoarding allowed. Once the new selections were made they were put into the class crate and returned to our classroom where the box sat underneath the teacher's desk until the next library time.

In the last year of Junior school another girl and I were appointed as library monitors for the whole school. This involved going to the library cupboards in the corridor to tidy the books. We had to make sure the books were standing to attention with their spines displayed outwards ready for the next class to make their choices on swapping day. This meant we were entrusted with the keys to the book cupboards. The other girl was bookish too and we started tidying the books every playtime; lunchtimes as well if we thought we could get away with it. We made a couple of piles of books on the floor in the corridor and then settled back with our current favourite to read a few more pages. And as long as the Headmaster was occupied in his office with the door shut this method worked well. We could enjoy several minutes of uninterrupted reading with the additional frisson of sudden discovery to add excitement to the thrill of the stories. It never occurred to either of us that our teachers knew exactly what we were up to and were delighted to have a couple of embryonic bookworms in the school.

One day, one of the lady teachers, the one who played the piano in assembly, saw us tidying the books and said that as we were so good at tidying she had another job for us. She told us we were to go into the staff room at the end of playtime and lunchtime. We were to wash up the cups and saucers, dry them and put them away in the cupboard above the sink; then wipe out the ashtrays; fold up the newspapers; plump up the cushions on the armchairs; and, unless it was raining, open the top window. We were delighted, as you can imagine. But even better she said that at the end of the week each of us would be paid one shilling for our efforts. Would we be willing to do this?

Would we be willing?

Willing Shilling!

And the dots joined up. Willing Shilling at Brownies was to earn money for the organisation but Willing Shilling at school was to keep for yourself!

Our Junior school was housed in a Victorian elementary school building: red-brick, slate roof, surrounded by black asphalt. The windows were too high for children to either see in or out of and there was a brick wall at the edge of the playground with ornate wrought iron gates. There were separate entrance doors for Boys, Girls and Infants but they were a hangover from earlier days and were now ignored as the infants had their own newly built school nearby.

Despite the organisational changes of the 1945 Education Act, which had sent the over elevens off to secondary modern school, the timetable hadn't changed much from the heyday of the three "Rs". First, every morning, we had Arithmetic, then assembly, followed by break-time. After break it was English which was divided into comprehension, spelling, dictation and composition taught separately on different days of the week. The afternoons were for subjects other than Arithmetic and English such as Nature, History and Art.

Once a week we went to the school hall for P.T. which meant Physical Training. In the classroom we removed our top layer of clothes and changed our shoes for a pair of "pumps" bought from Woolworths. Then, wearing only our vest and knickers, socks and pumps, we marched to the school hall where we were given bend and stretch type exercises to warm up. Next, we were issued with a small rubber mat to sit, stand or lie on while we did a few basic gymnastic moves. These included forward rolls (which we called "tipple-over-tails"), headstands and cartwheels. The lesson ended with running on the spot and marching round the room while stirring music was played on the record player.

The record player was a new addition to the school resources and sat on a high shelf attached to a large loudspeaker positioned further up the wall. The amplification was good, particularly for hearing the scratches on the records which crackled and hissed louder than the band playing the tunes.

In the summer the mats were put away and we had country dancing which was done in the playground if it was sunny. Summer was also the season for "Sports" culminating in the annual "Sports Day" where our athletic prowess was demonstrated in various races: running races; skipping races for the girls and sack races for the boys; potato races and egg-and-spoon races for the adroit and dextrous; relays for the grand finale. I never won any of these races but I was once picked for the school relay team at the District Sports: only because the fastest runners were off sick. Unsurprisingly, our team finished last.

Sports Day was one of the few occasions when parents were invited into school. They could also join in the Christmas Carol Concert and various other services held in the neighbouring church for Ash Wednesday, Ascension Day and Harvest Festival.

Our mum always came to school events when invited. One year our class did a Christmas play. I was given a speaking part and was very excited. Both my parents had been keen on amateur dramatics when they were younger and so they were excited too. On the day of the school performance, my mum arrived in good time and bagged herself a seat on the front row of the audience. Our class play commenced and it was soon time for my theatrical debut. One child was disguised as a snowman and a boy called Peter and I had to pretend to build it. This took all of ten seconds and then I was supposed to turn to Peter and say:

"Peter, Peter. Run and get a pipe of daddy's."

By now I was so excited at seeing my mum in the audience I completely forgot my line and stood staring out in silence. An exasperated prompt from the teacher reminded me of what to say and I whispered my line and exited stage left as quickly as possible. Thus ended my first and only starring role and nothing would ever persuade me to try acting again until many, many years later. I'm sure this must have been a great disappointment to my amateur thespian parents but they just said, "You were wonderful, darling," and left it at that.

Parents were expected to attend school medicals and any summons from the class teacher or Headmaster if something was wrong. My mum was once sent for by the class teacher who had something of importance to discuss. I was given a note about the appointment to take home. My mum went into panic mode, questioning me about what I'd done wrong. When I denied that anything was wrong she said they wouldn't have sent for her unless I'd transgressed. In fact, the teacher wanted to tell her why I wasn't doing very well at school. He'd discovered that I couldn't see the blackboard properly from the back of the class (where all the well behaved girls were made to sit) and he wondered if I needed an eye test. Meanwhile, he told her, he'd moved me to the front and had noticed a considerable improvement in my school work already.

My mum was mortified that she hadn't noticed this emerging problem as she punctiliously ensured our eyes were tested regularly. She immediately made an appointment at the optician's and, sure enough, glasses were prescribed. The optician recommended NHS children's specs as they were robust and free of charge. The lenses were small and round and encased in a salmon pink wire frame with curled wire to go round the ear. They were hideous and guaranteed to get all wearers called "specky-four-eyes" by those with twenty-twenty vision. The teacher continued to let me sit at the front of the class and I quickly learned to keep the specs in my desk and put them on only when absolutely necessary.

Overall, parental involvement in school was kept to an absolute minimum. The few parents who collected their children from school actually had to wait outside in the street. Crossing the school threshold was by invitation or appointment only. How different from today!

One afternoon each week we had Nature. Our teacher brought flowers, twigs and sea shells for the nature table and invited us to contribute too. Everything on the nature table was identified and labelled. The purpose of Nature Studies was to memorise the names of trees, flowers, birds, insects, bits of rock and woodland animals. The nature table was augmented by posters and a BBC schools radio programme about nature.

Learning all these nature names was assisted by out of school activities such as collecting Brooke Bond tea cards. These useful cards were first inserted into tea packets in 1954. Every time a new packet of tea was opened there was a search for the card and excited anticipation to see if it would be a new one or a duplicate of a card already collected. On lucky days there might be two cards in the packet! For sixpence an album was available into which the cards were glued. The first series of picture cards Brooke Bond produced was British Birds. The text was written and illustrated by an eminent naturalist, Frances Pitt, and collecting the cards became immediately popular. After a couple of years the renowned painter Charles Frederick Tunnicliffe became the Brooke Bond artist. Tunnicliffe had been brought up on a farm, experiencing the countryside at first hand, before he gained a scholarship to the Royal College of Art. He specialised in depicting birds and natural scenes in a variety of media including water colour, oils and engraving. The first Tunnicliffe series of Brooke Bond tea cards was a set of bird portraits and the cover of the album bore a greyscale sketch of a bird of prey. Subsequent Tunnicliffe collections included wild flowers, astronomy, fish, butterflies and African and Asian wild life.

The cards became so successful and popular that seven hundred and twenty million were distributed each year. Some children used the cards for "flixies" which was played up against a wall. If a flicked card landed on top of a card which had already been flicked it passed into the possession of a new owner. Naturally this lead to considerable arguments and disputes. We didn't play "flixies" with our cards because they were too precious; although we did do "swapsies" occasionally.

By the time a tea card album was complete a good knowledge of the subject matter could be acquired. However, a magnifying glass was needed to read the tiny print on the reverse of the cards. For more help with nature identification there were the "News Chronicle" I-Spy books. Titles included: I-Spy Birds; I-Spy Wild Flowers; I-Spy Butterflies and Moths; I-Spy Wild Fruits and Fungi; I-Spy Trees; and I-Spy Insects. Each of the I-Spy Nature books cost one shilling and included drawings and information relevant to the title. The idea was that you kept your eyes open and once something had been spotted it was recorded in the I-Spy book and points were collected. For sixpence there was a further extensive series including I-Spy At the Seaside; In the Country; In the Street; On a Farm; On a Train Journey; Dogs; Horses and Ponies; At the Zoo; The Sights of London; Ships and Harbours; Boats and Waterways; Aircraft; Cars; People and Places; and Musical Instruments. So many items to be on the look-out for it's a wonder my sister and I didn't suffer from stiff necks and eye strain!

Once completed, with everything in the book observed and recorded, the I-Spy book was posted off to "Big Chief I-Spy". This was to claim a certificate, a feather, and admittance to "The Redskins" as I-Spy followers were known. The concept of the I-Spy books was devised by a head teacher named Charles Warrell who self-published the books and appointed himself as the first Big Chief I-Spy. Mr Warrell's books were then taken over by the News Chronicle and briefly by The Daily Mail. Mr Warrell continued as Big Chief I-Spy until his retirement in 1956. He was succeeded as the Big Chief by Arnold Cawthrow, an Islington antiques dealer, who held the post until 1978. The newspaper sold on its ownership of the I-Spy books to other companies but publication ceased altogether in 2002. However, the I-Spy books were re-launched by Michelin a few years later. Mr Warrell, the originator and first Big Chief I-Spy, eventually went to the Happy Hunting Ground in 1995 aged one hundred and four. One hundred and four is an amazing age. Did his interest in observation increase his longevity? We'll never know.

We never actually managed to complete any of our I-Spy books so we couldn't send off for the feather and certificate. But the books were good fun and contributed considerably to our general knowledge. However, it was still possible to join The Redskins by sending sixpence to the News Chronicle. An I-Spy membership badge was issued in return together with a code book to decode Big Chief I-Spy's messages in his column in the newspaper.

The Redskins greeting was "How!" and at the start of the code book was a message from the Chief:

"HOW! and a warm welcome to I-Spy.

You have been initiated into the great tribe and I give you the right to use the secret codes and secret sign. The tribal rules tell you what is expected of all true Redskins. As chief of the I-Spy tribe I want to keep in touch with you. Through the News Chronicle you will receive the I-Spy passwords and my secret messages. I shall tell you of the doings of the great tribe. And from you I would like to hear of your I-Spying."

Then, as a taster for the exciting coded messages that were to be expected in the newspaper, the letter concluded:

"Odhu/ntinggo Redskin".

If you weren't a Redskin, there's a translation at the end of this book!

A new Redskin was exhorted to keep the codes secret and to keep the code book in a safe place; to use the secret sign and greeting if other Redskins were encountered; and to do some I-Spying every day. I certainly attempted to do some I-Spying every day but I never encountered any other Redskins except, of course, my younger sister.

Learning all the nature names in the I-Spy books could be very useful both at school and at Brownie meetings. Sometimes there were quizzes at Brownies where Brown Owl, or her assistant Tawny Owl, brought pictures or even the real thing for identification games. And at school, periodically, when the nature table was cleared the teacher would set a test to check if we could remember the names of the items.

Learning facts by rote was a big feature of the teaching style of the era. We learned our times tables to twelve x twelve along with the avoirdupois of weights and measures. I've never forgotten that there were one hundred and twelve pounds in one hundredweight and twenty hundredweights in one ton. Also that there were twenty two yards in one chain and ten chains in a furlong. Yet in the whole of my life it's never been necessary to use them!

We also knew from memory the words of the hymns we sang in assembly: from the hills of the north to the green hill far away. And in the last year of Junior school we learned poems with the aim of winning the prize for the pupil who could remember the most lines. I tried hard to win and knew Daffodils (twenty four lines); Meg Merrilies (thirty lines); Tyger, Tyger (twenty four lines; and the first five verses of The Ancient Mariner (twenty lines). But that wasn't enough to win.

The other significant teaching method was copying. This was different to copying the answers that a child sitting in a neighbouring seat wrote in a test. For that there was big trouble! No, this was copying what the teacher had previously chalked out on the board for the subject of the lesson. Usually this consisted of a picture pinned to the chalkboard or sketched out by the teacher with a few explanatory sentences written beneath: a bible story for religious education, an exotic fruit such as a pineapple for Geography or one of the items from the nature table which was all we did for Science.

Learning off by heart and copying were the mainstays of teaching methodology except for History where we had a textbook: the wonderful "Looking at History" series by R.J. Unstead. "From Cavemen to Vikings" in Junior One; "The Middle Ages" in Junior Two; "The Tudors and Stuarts" in Junior Three; and "From Queen Anne to Queen Elizabeth II" in Junior Four. First published in 1953 and re-published in 1961, these volumes brought a whole new way of learning history into our lives. The books were filled with detailed line drawings

18

and even had some beautiful full colour illustrations too. Written from a social history perspective, it was the stated aim of the author to make history come alive for the reader.

R.J. Unstead trained as a teacher at Goldsmiths' before the War. On the outbreak of war he joined the RAF and became a P.T. instructor. He subsequently served in Operations Control for the Normandy landings before further service in France, Greece and Italy. After resuming his teaching career he was appointed as head teacher of a school in Hertfordshire and started work on his history books. Writing eventually became his full time occupation with millions of copies of his books sold worldwide.

Our school copies of "Looking at History" were shared one between two; they were well-used, soft-backed and dog-eared. One Christmas I received, for a present, a new hard-backed copy of Book Two: The Middle Ages. The book had a colour picture of a jousting tournament on the cover and a paper dustjacket to keep it pristine. Inside was some memorable history including the excruciating section on crime and punishment.

I loved the irony of ordeal by fire as described by R.J. Unstead. The accused had to carry a piece of red-hot iron for three paces. Then the man's hand was bandaged and left for three days. In the unlikely event that there were no blisters when his hand was unwrapped, the accused was innocent. If blisters had formed he was punished or killed. Even better was ordeal by water where the accused was tied up and thrown into the river. If he floated he was guilty! R.J. Unstead's graphic accounts and the line drawings of the stocks, the pillory, the ducking stool and the scold's bridle left nothing to the imagination.

Included in the books were some sections called "Happenings" where the main events of history were detailed. R.J. Unstead's style was simple and direct. For example, he described Edward I as "...a strong king who restored order. He conquered Wales, for the Welsh people had never obeyed the Normans, and he built some fine castles like Harlech". My copy of The Middle Ages was thrown away long ago but I hankered to read it again. I ordered a copy from a second hand book dealer on Amazon and wallowed in the well-remembered pages. My newly acquired version of Looking at History is hard-backed and has five books all together in the one volume. The Queen Anne book of my childhood now ends at the death of Queen Victoria and there is a new fifth book entitled "The Twentieth Century". Not bad for just 1p plus postage and packing!

The volume was published in 1975 and has many more colour illustrations than the originals. Inside the fly-leaf is written:

"To Charles

From Nan and Bampy."

I hope Charles had as many hours of pleasure from his R.J. Unstead as I did.

Although treasured, my R.J. Unstead had to share my affections with a small collection of Puffin paperbacks. These were "The Secret Garden" and "The Little Princess" by Frances Hodgson Burnett; "Ballet Shoes" by Noel Streatfield; and "The Family from One End Street" by Eve Garnett. My favourite Puffin book, which I read over and over again, was "The Silver Sword" by Ian Serraillier.

Puffin paperbacks originated as non-fiction children's books in the 1930s and were so named to reflect the Penguin and Pelican titles published for adults by the Allen Lane company. The first Puffin fiction book, published in 1941, was "Worzel Gummidge" by Barbara Ephraim Todd. Paper shortages in the forties curtailed book publication but in the early fifties Puffin brought out C.S. Lewis' "The Lion, the Witch and the Wardrobe" and E.B. White's "Charlotte's Web". In 1961, Kaye Webb became the editor of Puffin books and started a golden age in publishing for children. The Puffin catalogue rose from one hundred and fifty one titles at the start of her regnum to one thousand two hundred and thirteen by 1969. Years later, when I became a primary school teacher, I occasionally read aloud my favourite books to the pupils at story time. I found I enjoyed the books just as much.

I also received a few hard-back books for Christmas and birthday presents. A favourite was the first "Bobbsey Twins" story by Laura Lee Hope. The story centres on a middle class, North American family with two sets of twins: Nan and Bert aged about twelve and Flossie and Freddy aged about six. I loved the opening of the book where the children are all sitting round the dining room table making a miniature house out of a cardboard box and creating the furniture and furnishings for the house from bits of cardboard cuttings. It inspired me to spend many a happy hour doing the same and also dressing peg dolls to live in the house. What I didn't know at the time was that the Bobbsey Twins books were written by a syndicate of writers. They started in the early years of the twentieth century and in the fifties and sixties up-dated and re-published the Bobbsey Twins series. The writers were known collectively as the Stratemeyer Syndicate and they also wrote the Nancy Drew mysteries. This syndicate of writers dominated American children's book publishing for decades. Despite their popularity, many libraries refused to stock the books because they weren't considered literature.

The same attitude was displayed in some parts of the UK to the prolific and highly readable Enid Blyton. My own favourites were the "Famous Five" books. I enjoyed spending time with Ann, Julian, Dick, George and Timmy, sharing their adventures, putting the world to rights and avoiding any dealings with the bad-tempered Uncle Quentin. Fortunately, the library we went to didn't hold any snobbish views. There were plenty of Famous Five titles, and other Enid Blyton books too, although the waiting time for some of them was considerable.

Occasionally our usual school timetable was suspended for something special. A couple of times each year there was a visit from the local council's road safety team accompanied by a member of Her Majesty's Constabulary. They came to school to remind us about crossing the road safely as there were some busy main roads in the vicinity. To help make us more traffic conscious, the road safety team were assisted by a friendly, little red squirrel called Tufty Fluffytail and his friends, Minnie Mole and Willy Weasel. Created in 1953 by Elsie Mills for the Royal Society for the Prevention of Accidents, these little cartoon characters became very popular, particularly after 1961 when the Tufty Club was started. Special road safety films were shown to Tufty Club audiences and we were also given badges, notebooks, pencils and handkerchiefs printed with road safety messages.

Harvest Festival was another big annual event in the school's calendar. On the day, we were asked to bring a decorated shoe box containing some fresh garden produce or eggs or tinned goods. These were displayed all day in the local church and then distributed by the vicar and his helpers to elderly folk in the neighbourhood who were deemed to be worthy recipients.

Twice a year the school held a "shoddy" collection when families were requested to send in old jumpers and cardigans or anything else made from wool. This was weighed and the school remunerated according to how much had been sent in. The garments were taken to woollen mills in the area and re-cycled into new fabric. This process, invented in the 1860s in Batley, produced an inferior woollen yarn by shredding scraps of the woollen garments into fibres. The fibres were mixed with small amounts of new wool to create the new product. Any wool which was unusable for shoddy was spread out onto the fields as manure!

The shoddy collection wasn't the only activity we undertook without realising we were saving the planet. As well as rinsing and putting out the milk bottles every day, we took lemonade or 'pop' bottles back to the shop and received a penny in return. Any old iron was handed over to the rag-and-bone man who came round the streets regularly with his horse and cart. He would pay for anything metal, no matter how rusty. He also took old clothes, blankets, coats and anything that wasn't wanted any more. Vegetable peelings, tea leaves and egg shells went into the compost pile at the bottom of the garden. Packaging was minimal and most shopping went straight into the basket or, if necessary, a paper bag. Fish and chips were wrapped in newspaper and old newspapers were used to light the fire. Unfortunately, the green-dream stops here as the fire was coal and heavily polluting, especially when mixed with fog that caused death inducing "smog". Clothes were repaired, buttons sewn back and holes in socks were darned. "Reduce - Re-use - Re-cycle" wasn't a slogan: it was a way of life!

However, most of our school days continued with predictable regularity. We knew exactly which lessons we'd be having and exactly the time of day we'd be having them for the whole of the school year: from September to July.

ELEVEN PLUS

I was nine years old when the new decade began. Of course, we didn't know on January 1st, 1960 that the Swinging Sixties had started. That came later. We didn't celebrate New Year's Eve in any special way. No-one came round to our house after midnight offering lumps of coal or a wee dram. As far as I know, my parents went to bed at the same time as usual. My dad had to go to work the next day and he didn't want to be late. A public holiday for New Year's Day wasn't introduced until 1974.

Most years we went to stay at our grandparents' house in the days between Christmas and New Year and the visit always ended with Happy New Year wishes and extra pocket money. Before that there was a family party when we would sit in grandma's front room where she had her best furniture and ornaments. We were forbidden to move in case we knocked anything over or spilt something on her square of best carpet. Not fitted carpet, just a square of Axminster in the middle of the room with an edging of linoleum fake floorboards.

As the evening went on my younger sister and I would gravitate towards the tiny scullery-kitchen at the back of the house where there was a large walk-in pantry with a marble slab to keep food cool. We took a couple of cushions and made a little den under the slab-shelf next to a crate of Eighty Plus. These were small bottles of fizzy orange juice that our great aunt Mary brought to the party from the brewery and soft drinks supplier where she worked. The bottles were dark brown with beer-bottle tops which we flicked off, saving the tops to play with later. We drank several bottles of Eighty Plus and ate our way through the Selection Boxes we'd received for Christmas. Eventually our mum would remember we hadn't gone to bed. She would track us down and send us off with a hot water bottle and exhortations to "go to sleep" which we quickly did. Only to wake up a couple of hours later when one or other of us threw up all over the bed. Poor mum! She spent so many Boxing Day nights washing bed-clothes and berating us for being so greedy.

At grandma's we had sheets and blankets with a feather eiderdown on top and sometimes a candlewick bedspread too. We wore winceyette nighties but even if we kept our dressing gowns on in bed we were cold. I once heard TV presenter Michael Parkinson reminiscing about his youth and he said that whatever might have been lacking in his up-bringing it wasn't warmth. In a coal-mining family, he said, their house was always toasty. Well, not in a railway worker's house in a neighbouring village it wasn't! And my other grandad was a retired coal miner who received an annual allowance of fuel but I don't re-call his tiny home being any warmer than anyone else's.

Usually on one of the days between Christmas and New Year we went to the pantomime at the "Alhambra" theatre in Bradford. However, one year we went to see a children's musical play at the "Playhouse" in Sheffield. My younger sister was deemed too young to come with us and had to stay at home with our auntie as baby-sitter. We sat in the dress circle at the Playhouse and shared the opera glasses that were mounted on the backs of the seats in front of us. They were ours for the duration of the play if a sixpence was inserted into the slot. They were particularly good for I-Spying members of the audience during the interval. The programmes were two and six (two shillings and sixpence) which my mum thought was extortionate. Two and sixpence in today's money is actually only twelve and a half pence, or one eighth of a pound. In the late 1950s one pound had the value of about twenty two pounds today. In 1957, my dad earned seven hundred and ninety nine pounds a year before income tax, his National Insurance stamp and pension contributions were deducted, so two and six for a theatre programme was a luxury!

I particularly enjoyed the play at Sheffield because it incorporated several songs including the memorable "Listen to the Wind" which was also the play's title. The play was originally produced at the Oxford Playhouse in 1954. The director was Peter Hall and a certain Ronald Barker (who later became famous in TV's "Open All Hours" and "Porridge") was one of the actors; as was Miriam Karlin who achieved success in "The Rag Trade". In 1955 "Listen to the Wind" transferred to the Arts Theatre in London's West End when Peter Hall went there as the artistic director. At the Arts, Hall was lauded for his direction of the first English speaking production of Samuel Beckett's "Waiting for Godot". A young Margaret Smith also joined the cast of "Listen to the Wind". As Maggie Smith she won the Best Actress Oscar in 1969 for "The Prime of Miss Jean Brodie" and gave an unforgettable performance as Lady Grantham in "Downton Abbey".

I don't know who acted in the version of "Listen to the Wind" that we saw at Sheffield: the over-priced programme was long since thrown away. The play was written by Angela Ainley Jeans with music by Vivian Ellis who'd had a successful career composing for light comedy musicals. "Listen to the Wind" was updated and revived in the 1990s at the "King's Head" theatre in London. Vivian Ellis wrote three new songs for the show but unfortunately died before the opening night.

Our great aunt who supplied the Eighty Plus at Christmas also occasionally provided us with a car on loan. My dad maintained that he'd learned to drive during his war service and he'd acquired a driving licence on demobilisation. He used his war gratuity to buy a small, three-wheeler, open-topped car rather like a souped-up Robin Reliant which he sold when I was born. Dad had a passion for English country churches. When he gratefully borrowed Auntie Mary's car for a day out we often visited one or two villages. He made straight for the church where we learned about clerestories, transepts, flying buttresses, gargoyles and other features of medieval church architecture. Our dad was particularly fond of Yorkshire's glorious ruined abbeys such as Rievaulx, Fountains and Jervaulx and over the years we visited all of them. Our regular visits to Leeds often included a walk round Kirkstall Abbey.

Eighty Plus Aunt Mary gave us a forty five rpm record which became an all-time favourite. It was a promotional disc for a brand of brandy that had been sent to the brewery where she worked. A deep, sultry, accordion-accompanied, fake French voice would tell us that "here in the castle the walls are strong, the vaults are deep, the time is long," with a rousing chorus of "In the Castle of Cognac". We were word perfect and sang along with French accents that we thought were impeccable!

To further our French education, Aunt Mary supplied my parents with a bottle of French wine to drink with Christmas dinner. (Only a small glass for the children mind!) Apart from the Christmas sherry (Harveys Bristol Cream) and a small bottle of medicinal whisky, there were no alcoholic drinks in our house. My grandparents augmented their Christmas sherry (Emva Cream) with De Kuyper Cherry Brandy, Warnink's Advocaat and Lamb's Navy Rum, but for most of the year their house was teetotal too. Our Christmas "dinner wine" was ritually opened in advance to "breathe" as this was what Aunt Mary said had to be done. We took it in turns to read the French words on the label, translating as best we could. The wine was poured out sparingly in order to save some for another day. It was an oily, yellow colour with a sickly sweet taste and we thought it was highly over-rated. It was only years later that I learned that a French Sauternes is more likely to be drunk as a dessert wine and probably chilled too! The experience, however, never put me off drinking wine as an adult, I'm glad to say.

Aunt Mary had a sister called Edith who, like her, was unmarried. They lived and worked together but were complete opposites in appearance. Aunt Mary was thin and angular while Auntie Edith was rounder and buxom. Edith died from breast cancer aged fifty seven and everyone was very sad. In 1938, these two aunts had enabled our mother to attend the High School for Girls after she passed the Eleven Plus. By then, school fees for children who passed The Scholarship had been abolished. However, uniform, books and sports equipment were all compulsory and still had to be paid for. This put a grammar school education out of the reach of many young people who were otherwise deemed suitable for it; and retained the exclusivity of the schools concerned. But the aunts said that as they had no children of their own they would support my mum through High School, which they generously did for five years.

When I was eleven we lived in the West Riding of Yorkshire, on the outskirts of Wakefield. In most places the Eleven Plus was still used to decide, on the basis of examination papers in numeracy, verbal reasoning and reading comprehension, the life paths of the entire generation. However, the innovatory educationalist Sir Alec Clegg, Chief Education Officer of the West Riding County Council, had introduced a new system known as the "Thorne System" to determine the allocation of pupils to the grammar schools using teacher assessment only. The outcome was still the same: just a small minority of pupils were deemed eligible for grammar school and the remainder had to attend secondary modern school. However, the selection process was regarded as fairer under the Thorne System because it allowed children who were stressed out by the all-or-nothing pressure of the Eleven Plus Exam to still have a chance at entering the elite schooling system. As far as I know I'm one of the few children of that era who obtained a place at grammar school without actually taking the Eleven Plus.

I don't know what criteria the teachers used but I was allocated a place at the nearest grammar school. The only trouble was it was several miles away from where we lived. Starting at the school was a complete shock. I was used to catching the bus into town with my younger sister but to get to the grammar school I had to catch a public service bus along an unfamiliar route in the opposite direction. Several older pupils from the school used the bus too. It was one of the rituals of school life that, as the bus travelled along, new starters had their school uniform berets thrown out of the upper deck windows by the older pupils. The uniform was expensive and had to be purchased in Leeds at a specialist uniform suppliers. When my beret went out of the window it was getting dark outside and I hadn't a clue where I was. I was off the bus in a flash to retrieve the beret. I had to wait ages for the next bus and when I finally arrived home my mum was furious because the beret had mud on it. She wasn't a bit bothered about what the other kids had done and said I would have to learn to stand up for myself. That was all very well: she didn't have to go through the holly bush which was the other rite of passage inflicted on all we first-year innocents.

Although situated in an urban, built-up area, the school had extensive grounds which included trees and overgrown bushes. One of these bushes was a massive holly bush. At break and lunch times, new pupils were captured by older boys and girls and forced to walk through the holly bush. These more established pupils had themselves endured the initiation ceremony in previous years and were determined to see the tradition perpetuated. Obviously this scramble through the holly bush was more painful for the pupils who went through first. A few of the girls in my class, me included, were savvy enough to hide out in the toilets for a couple of days until the middle of the bush had a pathway worn through it and the ritual could be endured painlessly.

The other difficulty of starting secondary school was navigating the maze of corridors that connected the school's various teaching blocks. In the first week I found myself lost and had to pluck up the courage to open a door to one of the many rooms. I was horrified to find it full of fifteen and sixteen year olds and their teacher. In a faltering, nervous whisper I asked for directions to my classroom. A very tall girl with plaits wound round her head and a face full of freckles offered to take me to the right place. I've remembered her kindness all my life.

The Rothwell Grammar School was opened in the 1930s and has an interesting history. After the First World War, a group of Labour councillors on the West Riding County Council began to dream of establishing a grammar school to serve their area. Situated between Wakefield and Leeds the area included Lofthouse, Stanley, Ardsley East and Outwood. In 1925, a site for the new school became available when a local industrialist decided to sell off some land at Lofthouse Hall. Seventeen acres were purchased but because they were subject to coal mining subsidence the plans had to be put on hold until the land settled. Further delays were caused by the objections of central government officials who were not convinced of the need for another grammar school in the area. Their approval was required to allow the council to borrow the money to build the school. However the local Labour councillors persisted and the civil servants finally capitulated after being persuaded that an increasing child population warranted the investment. It may be that the election of Ramsey Macdonald's Labour government helped them change their minds too.

The school finally opened in 1933 and the Headmaster was Mr E. R. Manley. There were five other teachers and eighty one pupils. Mr Manley was still the Headmaster when I started attending the school in 1962 although he retired the next year.

In retirement, Mr Manley wrote a series of English text books in four volumes: "The Essence of English". He went to live in the Oxfordshire village of East Hendred. He became the Secretary of the Hendred's Society and wrote a village history book to celebrate the formation of the society. He was dissatisfied with the type setting of the book but died suddenly in 1970 before he was able to do anything about it.

Mr Manley was a socialist and member of the Labour Party. He was involved in local politics and became a Labour councillor representing the Lofthouse ward of the Rothwell Urban District Council. He was elected chairman of the library and housing committees and chairman of the full council for a year as well. Ironic that the parish church of this socialist's retirement village is where David and Samantha Cameron were married.

The Rothwell Grammar School motto was "Nec Spurno Nec Timeo" which we were soon to find out was Latin for "Neither do I spurn nor do I flee". Latin was my favourite lesson and we had a lovely textbook called "Latin is Fun". A previous user of my copy had altered the cover so that the title now read "Eating is Fun". I covered the book in brown paper and reinstated the title correctly. There wasn't much I could do about the flyleaf of the book on which someone had inscribed in commendably neat handwriting:

Latin is a dead language
As dead as it can be
It killed the mighty Romans
And now it's killing me.

My dad liked Latin too and presented me with my first Latin sentence to translate:

Caesar adsum iam forte. Cassius passus sum sed e.

This sentence made absolutely no sense whatsoever until, with a twinkle in his eye, my father informed me that the Latin letter 'j' is written with an English 'i'. It was, of course, dog Latin, which when read aloud in English pronunciation becomes: "Caesar had some jam for tea. Cassius, pass us some said he". Now you know why I've called this book of reminiscences "Jam for Tea".

We had Latin lessons every day and homework once a week. There was a list of vocabulary to learn and everything was arranged in a wonderful orderly manner. The teaching was systematic, repetitious and highly effective. In no time I knew some nouns and verbs and how to combine them in simple sentences. French was also taught with a daily lesson, weekly homework and frequent testing of vocabulary lists. I started to see the similarities between French and Latin and how lots of English words had Latin roots and I usually got twenty out of twenty for the vocabulary tests.

Other new subjects included Science lessons in the laboratories. The labs persistently had a faint smell of gas from the Bunsen burner taps to which daring pupils, when they thought no-one was looking, would give a little twist. Physical Education was hockey which needed shin pads and quick wits to avoid large bruises. Arithmetic became Maths which included Algebra and Geometry too.

The very best bit of Rothwell Grammar School was the Tuck Shop. It was open every morning break for the sale of Wagon Wheels, Chocolate Teacakes and packets of chocolate digestive biscuits. There may have been other delicacies on sale but these were the ones I bought every day until my pocket money ran out. Of course, the main meal of the day was school dinners but I've said all that needs saying about them in "Cabbage and Semolina"!

Once I'd found my way between home and school; learned to navigate the corridors; got used to the new lessons and forgotten about the initiation rites, I thought the school was great. But after I'd attended Rothwell Grammar School for just a couple of months my dad was appointed to a new job and moved our family to a small, country market town in Lincolnshire. There the grammar school used the Eleven Plus Examination to select its intake. My dad was anxious that I wouldn't be accepted because of the Thorne System. Fortunately, Sir Alec's teacher assessment innovation had the same currency as the formal exam and I was given a place. So again, I was able to enter grammar school without sitting the Eleven Plus. Thank you, Sir Alec!

OPERATION BRITAIN

A few weeks before leaving Junior school our class was given a special educational treat. We were presented with a copy of the "British Trades Alphabet" (BTA). This was an annual magazine that was given free to over a million school children aged between nine and fifteen years. The magazine gave information about a number of products and companies. As well as articles about subjects deemed to be of interest to the target audience, there was an alphabet of the products. Twenty six pages were headed with an alphabet letter and a rhyme for each of the twenty six products. There was information about the product, often in cartoon form, with details of how to find out more. In addition there were competitions to enter which included a handwriting competition and a project competition. For the project competition a product had to be chosen from one of those advertised in the magazine, researched further and a folder of information submitted to the magazine's publisher.

The page for Hovis bread appealed to me and further information was offered on receipt of a stamped addressed envelope. This proved to be a booklet describing the process of flour manufacture. The booklet contained samples of flour at each stage of production. The samples were packaged in tiny, opaque envelopes and stuck into the booklet on the appropriate page. A second stamped addressed envelope sent to Cadbury's resulted in a life size paper replica of a cocoa bean. This opened out to show, in full technicolour, a cross section through the bean. As I usually ate more bread than cocoa beans I chose bread for my project. I copied out all the information in the booklet in my best handwriting, added everything else I could think of about the subject, drew some pictures, traced a map or two and sent the project off in the hopes of winning a prize. I didn't win but it was good fun and I kept the flour samples (and the cocoa bean) for years.

Winning could be a reality for some though. There's a report in "The Yorkshire Post and Leeds Intelligencer" in November 1954, of a Leeds fifteen year old actually winning a prize in the BTA competition with her book, written in seven chapters, about bread. Jean, who was a pupil at Sandford Secondary Modern School, produced her book in two months of spare time study and writing. She told the newspaper she gained her information from books in the school and public libraries, from the local baker and also from other bakeries who sent her pamphlets describing their work. With her prize money she actually bought a gold watch! Jean was due to leave school in three weeks and as she was an obvious candidate for a career in bread production had accepted an invitation to visit a flour mill in Manchester. However, her ambition was to become a comptometer operator, which was the career destination of choice for many in pre-computer days. Looking at all Jean's hard work, it's no wonder my paltry effort didn't stand a chance.

The British Trades Alphabet was associated with the Commonwealth Trades Alphabet started in Australia and New Zealand in 1913. The magazine claimed a worldwide circulation of over four million. The British version was actually produced in Lofthouse near to where we lived, although the magazine was distributed all over the country. The magazine was not without controversy. There were strong objections by some local councillors and teachers to promoting advertising in schools. When the BTA was launched in 1953 some educationists viewed it as an advertising stunt. However, the distributors claimed the magazine had been welcomed by hundreds of teachers across the country. As well as being the head teacher of Rothwell Grammar School, Mr Manley was the press secretary for the West Yorkshire Association of the National Union of Teachers. He told the "Yorkshire Post" that he'd not actually seen a copy of the British Trades Alphabet but explained that many industrial firms sent out books and magazines containing useful information, often of a high standard. However, he was adamant that if there was an excess of advertising in the BTA it wouldn't be tolerated.

Recently I found a copy of the 1958 British Trades Alphabet for sale on Ebay and I asked my brother-in-law to bid for it. As no-one else was interested in this 1950s treasure he got it for just £1! It's slightly crumpled, stained and dog-eared round the edges but is very similar to the copy I was given at school. Some of the pages inside are identical to the pages I remembered from the version of the magazine I was given.

BSA Cycles had the 'B' page. Their rhyme was:

B stands for Birmingham

The home of BSA

Who make the finest bicycles

Upon the road to-day.

The BSA page included several line drawings depicting the history of the bicycle from the days of the "Hobby Horse" and the "Penny Farthing" to modern day cycles. These were described, in contrast to the earlier versions, as "attractive in appearance, safe and comfortable to ride." BSA are the initials of the Birmingham Small Arms company who, unsurprisingly, manufactured weapons during the nineteenth century. The company branched out into bicycle manufacture from the 1880s and later into motorcycles as well. In the late fifties the bicycle business was sold on to Raleigh.

My first bicycle - actually a tricycle - was made by BSA and had a little metal BSA label on the back of the saddle. The bike pedals were very stiff to rotate to get the thing going. It was painted completely black with just a shiny, silver bell on the handlebar to brighten it up. On the rare occasions I rode it in the street it usually ended up tipping over, causing scraped knees for me or whoever else was trying to ride it. However, the tricycle was very robust and I wouldn't be surprised to hear that it lasted for many years after my mum gave it away to some neighbour's children when we moved.

31

The Gas Council had the 'F' page in the BTA:

F is for Fuel that's smokeless and bright,

Mr Therm's gas and coke which make work so light,

And F's for the fabulous things he obtains

From coal at the Gasworks, to add to our gains.

The rhyme was accompanied by a line drawing of the inside of a house and its garden with an invitation to see how many things Mr Therm helped to create. The text advised the reader to look for twenty one items used in everyday life made from the materials produced when coal is turned into gas. Helpfully the answers were printed upside-down at the bottom of the page and included gas for the cooker and water heater; coke for the fire; tar for the street; petrol for the car; paints, perfumes, nylon, dyes, varnishes, drugs, detergents, food flavourings and disinfectant. Readers were offered more information in a free illustrated booklet that they could collect from the Gas Showroom. With it came a career opportunity: "Thousands of boys and girls enter the Gas Industry every year. There are lots of interesting jobs with excellent prospects".

Originally designed in 1932 by Eric Fraser for the Gas Light and Coke Company, Mr Therm was a well-established mascot for the whole of the gas industry by the fifties and sixties. He was very easy to draw and his androgynous form and "Little Weed" type face became a staple for decorating the covers of my school exercise books.

British Nylon Spinners had the 'N' page with a photo montage of items made from nylon for the reader to identify plus a free offer of an information sheet.

N is for Nylon, the yarn of to-day -

You see it at work, you see it at play.

Wherever you look you find nylon ahead

In hundreds of uses from A down to Z.

As girls we loved nylon frocks but the Spinners were also offering ribbon, teddy bears, tennis nets and racquets, fishing line and suitcases as examples of the versatility of nylon. Nylon was invented in the 1930s but the fifties saw the launch of Crimplene. This was a much thicker fabric than nylon and it was wrinkle resistant and kept its shape well. Crimplene became increasingly popular throughout the sixties. My mum bought a Crimplene dress to wear at a wedding reception. The room had several heaters round the perimeter and in the crush she was pushed against one. The dress immediately started scorching but fortunately she was able to move away before too much damage was done. She had to keep her back turned away from all the other guests for the remainder of the evening though, so no-one could see the large, brown scorch mark on her bottom.

Other companies who'd taken a page in the British Trades Alphabet were Outspan Oranges; Mentmore Manufacturing who produced the Platignum fountain pen; Cadbury's chocolate; the Dunlop Rubber company; Foster Clark's Eiffel Tower Orange and Lemonade drinks; Gibbs SR toothpaste; Basildon Bond stationery; Sirdar knitting wool; the National Milk Publicity Council; National Benzole; Lyons Tea; and The White Fish Authority. Just reading the names of these products evokes for me the social and commercial landscape of the 1950s. It's interesting to see which companies continue to trade and which have become lost in the passing of time.

The 'Q' page was devoted to Quality.

Q stands for Quality of each Morris car.

It's the reason why Morris have progressed so far.

You see Morris cars on the roads everywhere...

It's "Quality First" that has put them all there.

There followed a short history of road travel and drawings of the Morris Oxford and Morris Minor in their original designs from 1912 and 1930 respectively. These models had been re-designed and were still on sale, although the Morris Minor was re-branded as the Morris 1000. As for "Quality First", my dad bought a Morris 1000 in 1963 and while driving along a country road the gear stick came off in his hands but he just shoved it back in and continued on his journey. It's a good thing my mum wasn't with him at the time. She would have screamed out loud. She was a very nervous passenger and a terrible back-seat driver.

The introduction to the 1958 edition of the British Trades Alphabet was written by Lord Luke who was the Chairman of the British Advertising Association. In his remarks he encouraged the youth of Britain to aim high and to set their sights on university. Unbelievably, he wrote: "No boy or girl is denied a University education if merited." He went on: "Take your own school. Make a list of old boys and girls who went to Universities in the last five years. Your teacher will help you in this." Really! I suspect none; none; none; none; and none would have been the answer at my Junior school. His optimistic tone continued: "Even if circumstances force you to leave school at a much earlier age than you would like, remember that in industry there are great opportunities for further education and advancement." And he concluded, "And you can play your part in Great Britain's future which can still be great. There are fewer obstacles to your progress in the world today and there are still greater worlds to conquer in science, literature and, of course, space." Stirring stuff!

The previous year Lord Luke had been named as the Head of "Operation Britain" which was an advertising campaign launched to promote British manufacturing. It doesn't appear to have made much of an impact unlike the "I'm Backing Britain" campaign which sprang up ten years later.

My memory has somehow muddled up the "I'm Backing Britain" campaign with "World Cup Willy", probably because of the predominance of Union Jacks in both campaigns. The "I'm Backing Britain Campaign" was the brain-child of five secretaries working in the headquarters of a heating company in Surbiton. Nationally, there was a balance of payments deficit because imports hugely exceeded exports. The government had devalued the pound to try and increase exports after previously raising interest rates to 6% to no avail. A Member of Parliament wrote to "The Times" demanding that management should set a good example and work an extra half day for no additional pay to help the export drive. At the end of December 1967 the five secretaries at the heating company received a memo from their marketing director. This asserted that if all the workforce worked an extra half day for no extra pay the economic difficulties of the country could be sorted out. The secretaries responded by balloting their co-workers to start work on one day each week at eight thirty instead of nine o'clock. This was the starting point for the "I'm Backing Britain" campaign. The campaign was given lots of publicity in the press and spawned a single by Bruce Forsyth. It was reported by supermarkets, in due course, to have made no difference whatsoever to their profit margins. The sale of campaign T-shirts was compromised when it became known that the T-shirts had been manufactured in Portugal, hardly contributing to the export drive! By the end of 1968 the campaign had largely fizzled out.

"World Cup Willy" actually came before the "I'm Backing Britain Campaign" and was the mascot for England in the 1966 Football World Cup. It was the first really successful sports branding campaign. A mop-headed lion, always clad in red, white and blue, was featured on mugs, tea towels and bedspreads in a way that hadn't been seen before. The designer was a commercial artist called Reg Hoye, and he submitted four different designs to the campaign team. His lion, based on drawings of his son Leo, was selected to become "World Cup Willy". Maybe England should bring Willy out of retirement for 2018.

The back cover of my recently acquired British Trades Alphabet for 1958 has several colour images of trains and the heading "The Future is Bright for Careers on British Railways". The text explains that there had been "a reawakening to the importance of an efficient railway system" in the country with several innovations such as electrification, dieselisation and power signalling. This, it says, is the reason why there are many opportunities in the railway for the "right kind of boy and girl". Unfortunately, this surprising (for the 1950s) example of equal opportunities is not continued into the second paragraph where it's explained that the continued modernisation of British Railways is dependent on "a steady flow of keen, able and energetic young men" to keep the modernisation programme moving forwards. The page concludes with an invitation to readers to contact the Regional Staff Officer at the address provided for information about the many jobs available at British Railways. However, any dreams I might have had of following in my grandfather's footsteps and working on the railway would have been quashed when the first Beeching Report was published five years later. The report recommended that two thousand three hundred and sixty three stations and five thousand miles of track (55% and 30% respectively of the total) should be closed down.

As far as I am able to find out the company publishing the British Trades Alphabet went into liquidation in 1988. There don't seem to be many second hand copies available. If you've secreted one up in the loft or out in the garden shed I suggest you hang on to it. It might be valuable one day!

SWINGING SIXTIES

The Sixties didn't really start to swing until a few years into the decade. By the mid-sixties Twiggy, Mary Quant, Julie Christie, Sandie Shaw, Mick Jagger, Ray Davies, David Bailey, Ossie Clark and David Hockney (to name but a few) had defined the era in fashion, music, the arts and style. Swinging London had become the epicentre of global cool.

However, the start of the decade was just a continuation of the Fifties apart from a few momentous events. In 1961 the unbelievable happened. The Russians put a man into space. They'd already put a dog into orbit a few years previously to discover some of the problems that were likely to occur if they fired a human up there too. Laika, a husky-terrier cross, was a stray from the streets of Moscow who received the dubious honour of being selected to venture where no man had been before. The experiment, in Sputnik 2 on November 3rd 1957, was designed to test if a living creature could survive the challenges of the launch and subsequent weightlessness. The information gleaned was used in further developments to the Russian space programme.

Everyone was space mad. Well, at least the boys were. When, on April 12th 1961, Yuri Alekseyevich Gagarin, a Soviet pilot and cosmonaut, made the first successful manned orbit of the earth in his spacecraft Vostok the excitement was palpable. Now all the boys wanted to be astronauts and any one of them would have given their right arm to swap places with Major Gagarin.

Gagarin became a celebrity and was awarded countless honours both in Russia and elsewhere across the world. He continued to work in the Soviet space programme until his untimely death in a training accident in a MiG fighter in 1968. Laika, the dog, was even more unfortunate: she burned to death in the first hours of her space flight. This was kept secret for many years although we were told she'd survived for much longer. My younger sister, who loved dogs, was appalled. She didn't consider the technological discoveries to be sufficient justification for cruelty to the dog.

I was more impressed when, a couple of years later, the Russians decided to go one step further and put a woman into space. Out of hundreds of applicants Valentina Tereshkova, a worker in a textile factory, was selected. She was the right height and weight but most importantly had skills which were essential for the space training programme: she was a sky diver. Valentina was successfully launched into space on 16th June 1963. She orbited the earth forty eight times and stayed in space for almost three days. I still didn't want to be an astronaut but I was glad that a woman had shown she could do space travel too.

My family's other interest in the Russians occurred when John Ogden won the Moscow International Piano Competition in 1962. He shared the first prize with the Russian pianist, Vladimir Ashkenazy. Born in Nottingham in 1937, Ogden was only in his mid-twenties when he gained international acclaim. We'd watched him perform at a concert in the Town Hall in Leeds and were delighted when he won the Moscow prize, being the first Westerner to do so. On his return to the UK he performed at an extra special concert in the St. George's Hall, Bradford and my dad got tickets for me and him to attend. I've lost the programme but I'm sure Ogden played the Tchaikovsky piano concerto.

As well as John Ogden we'd seen performances by most of the top piano soloists of the day. Ashkenazy, Barenboim and Brendel stand out. Usually they played with the Halle Orchestra but sometimes it was the Birmingham Symphony Orchestra or the Bournemouth Symphony Orchestra. I don't re-call any women soloists, although my dad had been to several Myra Hess concerts when he was stationed in London during World War Two. As far as he was concerned there was no-one to match her. I was fortunate to get a ticket for Arthur Rubenstein playing Chopin at the Royal Festival Hall in the early seventies and I think his performance was the greatest I've ever heard.

As I became more proficient at piano playing, my dad bought some books of piano duets. He played the bottom part and I played the top. We tried to replicate, without much success, some of the classics we'd enjoyed in the concert halls. Our favourite duet was an adaptation of Faure's "Dolly Suite" which started with the piece made famous as the theme tune for "Listen with Mother". On my wedding day, my dad and I were alone and waiting for the ancient, hired Bentley to come and take us to the church. In our nervousness we ran out of things to talk about, so, he in his wedding suit and me in my frilly frock, sat and played our favourite duets until the car turned up.

In addition to the Moscow International Piano Festival, the Russians were also significant in our lives because of the Cold War. This reached a high point in October 1962 with the Cuban Missile Crisis. In the previous year the American CIA backed invasion of the Bay of Pigs failed. Then, on October 14th 1962, tension between the USA and the Soviet Union went stratospheric. Literally! The pilot of an American U-2 spy plane, making a high-altitude pass over Cuba, photographed a Soviet SS-4 medium-range ballistic missile being assembled for installation.

From the American point of view nuclear weapons only ninety miles from their border caused grave disquiet. The next few days were full of urgent diplomacy which culminated on October 22nd when President Kennedy addressed the American nation in a television broadcast. He said that a blockade of Cuba had been enacted and that he was prepared to neutralise the Soviet threat if necessary.

On October 24th 1962, Soviet ships heading for Cuba neared the line of US vessels enforcing the blockade. An attempt by the Soviets to breach the blockade would have sparked a military confrontation that could have quickly escalated into a nuclear war. But the Soviet ships stopped short at the blockade. The world waited for the Russian response.

Meanwhile, our dad had been promoted to a new job and on that same day, October 24th 1962, our family moved ninety miles south to a new home in Lincolnshire. Hardly an auspicious time for a move. As the world hovered on the brink of disaster, we sat in front of the fire in our new home, surrounded by packing cases, our mum holding us close as the clock on the mantelpiece ticked the hours away.

All the adults seemed nervous. Their anxiety communicated itself to us although they tried to pretend that nothing was wrong. Child though I was, I'll never forget my feelings then. It seemed as though everything in our safe, secure, familiar world was falling to pieces. Everything we knew in Wakefield had gone. All that seemed ahead of us was complete uncertainty in our own lives and in the fate of the world.

Fortunately, on October 26th, the Russian President Vladimir Khrushchev sent a message to Kennedy. He offered to remove the Cuban missiles in exchange for a promise by US leaders not to invade Cuba. Even though an American spy plane was shot down over Cuba the next day and American troops were assembled in Florida, Kennedy accepted the offer and the world breathed again. The two super-powers made some new diplomatic arrangements to avoid such a conflict in the future amongst which was a "hot-line" between Washington and Moscow to facilitate better communications. However the nuclear arms race continued and the whole of the Swinging Sixties was overshadowed by the Cold War nuclear threat. Perhaps that's why the youth became so anti-establishment and didn't trust anyone over thirty.

We felt closer to America after the launch of the first Telstar satellite. This created an occasional link for television and telephone communications between Europe and North America.

Of course, we were already accustomed to European television links. As a family we'd been watching the Eurovision Song Contest since the fifties. For Britain, Pearl Carr and Teddy Johnson came second in 1959 with "Sing Little Birdie" although the UK didn't have a winning song until Sandie Shaw sang "Puppet on a String" (barefoot) in 1967.

The Telstar satellite was launched on July 10th 1962 and relayed its first public broadcast a couple of weeks later. The satellite signal was available earlier than anticipated so President Kennedy was unable to broadcast to Europe as planned. Fortunately, Richard Dimbleby was in Brussels standing by for the occasion. This was a momentous event and I wanted to wait up to see the first television pictures ever transmitted from America but they didn't come through until the early hours of the morning and by then I'd gone to bed and so I missed it.

Dimbleby had been the leading news commentator for the BBC since he described to the nation the funeral of King George VI and the coronation of Elizabeth II. His sepulchral tones were the voice of Britain on all state occasions including Churchill's funeral in 1965. We all watched the funeral on television. We were very impressed with the scale of the event and especially the ending. When the barge carrying Churchill's coffin back to his ancestral home in Oxfordshire passed through the London docks the cranes were lowered in a gesture of respect. Richard Dimbleby himself died later that same year.

Friday November 22nd 1963.

Were you there when the terrible announcement of President Kennedy's assassination was made? We'd just had our tea and my younger sister and I were sitting with our mum, who was heavily pregnant, when we heard the news. We were all shocked and began to cry. Since his election in November 1960, television, magazines and newspapers had been filled with photos of the new, dynamic President, his wife and young family. We didn't understand the ins and outs of American politics but we were impressed by his inaugural speech which famously included, "ask not what your country can do for you, but what you can do for your country". The drama of Kennedy's death and the subsequent capture and murder of his assassin dominated the TV News until eventually the far less charismatic Lyndon B. Johnson was sworn in to re-place Kennedy.

Although we watched the News every evening, more often than not it was in the background for me and my younger sister. In the fifties we just watched Children's Hour and a few programmes our parents approved of like "Dixon of Dock Green". On Saturday nights at five past six we always watched the BBC's first attempt at a pop music show, "Six Five Special" presented by Pete Murray and Josephine Douglas. The exciting steam train introduction - "over the points - over the points" was sung by the programme's resident band, Don Lang and the Frantic Five. We thought the driver in the locomotive cab looked like our railway engine driver grandad but it wasn't. We always joined in with the words of the song: "The Six Five Special's coming down the line, the Six Five Special's right on time," and waited in anticipation for Pete Murray's introduction: "It's time to jive on the old six-five" in a fake transatlantic twang. That was usually the end of the excitement because the show was mainly ballads. After a while my sister and I would wander off and go and play in the front sitting room.

ITV started a pop music programme aimed specifically at teenagers. This was called "Oh Boy!" and Cliff Richard and The Shadows were regulars along with Marty Wilde. The various guest singers were often accompanied by the resident band, Lord Rockingham's Eleven. We loved "Hoots Mon" and the brilliant Cherry Wainer. The screaming kids in the audience and the big frocks of The Vernon Girls were a lot more exciting than the old six-five. Sadly, we didn't get to watch "Oh Boy!" very often: our parents wouldn't allow it but we saw the show occasionally if we were at someone else's house.

In 1959, the BBC began to broadcast "Juke Box Jury". The "jury" comprised four celebrity guests who decided on the hit potential of some recently released records. The show was hosted by David Jacobs who played the records on his juke box and asked the jurors to decide if it would be a hit (bell rung) or a miss (loud hooter). In the event of a tie three members of the audience would hold up a "Hit" or "Miss" disc. The show was very popular and regularly reached an audience of over twelve million viewers. It ran for several years before being axed in 1967. I usually watched the show but thought that lots of the comments made about the songs by the jury were biased. I couldn't stand the irritatingly smooth presenter either so I wasn't sorry when it went off air.

However, it wasn't long before new music shows were launched and the Swinging Sixties became the golden age of pop music programming!

"Oi'll give it foive," said Janice Nicholls, one of the three teenagers who joined a guest DJ to review new singles on the ABC music show "Thank Your Lucky Stars". The show started in 1961 and was introduced by Brian Matthews. There were both British and American acts who usually mimed to their records. The more well known the act, the more songs they performed. This meant the Fab Four and other top performers sang as many as four songs. "Thank Your Lucky Stars" was the first time that ordinary teenagers like Janice Nicholls were having their views listened to and taken seriously. The spending power of youthful baby boomers was on the increase and the latest 45s were one of the biggest must-haves of the day. Janice started a catch-phrase. For several months my sister and I and just about every other child we knew would show our approval of anything by saying, "Oi'll give it foive".

Then, on Friday evening, 9th August 1963 the world changed. This was the night the greatest pop music show ever created commenced. "Ready Steady Go!" hit our screens. Now this was something different. In addition to the main studio area, the singers performed on mini-stages and the stairs. There was close contact between the groups and the audience. The teenagers who were lucky enough to be present at the recording of the show were seen dancing to every song. "RSG!" was pop music heaven.

The show started off with Manfred Mann's "5-4-3-2-1" although other songs were used for the introduction at different times. The main presenters were DJ Keith Fordyce and later Cathy McGowan. Originally employed in fashion at "Woman's Own", McGowan applied to be an adviser on "Ready Steady Go!" and was offered a presenting job. Of a similar age to the audience, McGowan's iconic long dark hair, heavy fringe and black eye makeup soon became (along with the music) the main reason for watching.

I wanted to look like Cathy but unfortunately my hair was short, blonde and slightly curly. This was very frustrating until a couple of years later when Lesley Hornby burst onto the scene. With her short, blonde, close cropped hair, Twiggy was a role model I could copy. I had my hair cut into her trademark style but unfortunately my natural curls made the sides stick out. First I tried using metal pin curlers to make the sides stay flat. Every time I turned over in my sleep the curlers stuck into my face and woke me up. They didn't work either and the wayward curls persisted. So, I resorted to strips of sellotape to stick down the sides and this worked just fine. Except that every morning I set off for school with a livid red rectangle on each cheek where the sellotape had been pulled off. But the mark had usually gone by about ten o'clock so I thought it was well worth it.

"Ready, Steady Go!" was cancelled for unknown (and to me devastating) reasons in 1966. The show had become a bone of contention between me and my parents. My dad was normally a mild mannered and gentle man but the sight of the increasingly long-haired youths in the pop groups sent him into apoplexies. He was particularly exercised by Mick Jagger and joined the army of men of his generation who discovered a yearning for "short back and sides" and National Service.

The BBC's "Top of the Pops" started a few months after RSG! and ran until 2006. I was never a big fan of TOTP preferring to listen to the charts on the radio on Sunday afternoon with Alan Freeman's "Pick of the Pops". There are frequent re-runs of old recordings of TOTP on BBC4 but I've never found anything similar on ITV for "Ready Steady Go!"

Our family's first pop record was "Walking Back to Happiness" sung in 1961 by Helen Shapiro, although we'd already got a copy of Tommy Steele singing "Little White Bull" from the 1959 film "Tommy the Toreador". This extraordinary film, in which a sailor from Liverpool disembarks in Spain and becomes a bull fighter, also starred Sid James, Janet Munro and Bernard Cribbins. We saw the film at "The Regal" cinema in Wakefield and loved every minute of it. We were word perfect in "Little White Bull" but there was a much better Tommy Steele song, "Singing Time", on the B side.

We didn't go to the cinema very often but we were taken to see Hayley Mills in her first Disney role as Pollyanna in the 1960 film of the same title. Based on the children's novel written in 1913 by Eleanor Porter, the film told the story of poor orphaned Pollyanna who was forced to live with her rich, strict and unloving aunt. However, Pollyanna's never ending optimism gains her countless friends in her new community. The sickly, saccharine film gained Hayley Mills an Academy juvenile award for her performance along with a BAFTA nomination. We liked the film a lot and, for a while, became big fans of Hayley Mills. We especially enjoyed her singing "Let's Get Together" (yeah, yeah, yeah) in her 1961 film "The Parent Trap" and we were quickly word perfect in singing along with that one too.

Of course Yeah, Yeah, Yeah would be the catch phrase of the Swinging Sixties. From The Beatles "She Loves You" (yeah, yeah, yeah) to Georgie Fame and The Blue Flames "Yeah Yeah" no song was complete without a yeah or two.

The first record I bought for myself was the 1962 "Let's Dance" sung by Chris Montez with "You're the One" on the B side. I played it so many times the needle wore out on the gramophone; or at least that was the reason my dad gave me when he banned it. He was very picky about the quality of the stylus for his classical records and said he didn't want his collection damaged. I suspect, however, he was sick of the monotonous beat of "Let's Dance". He was giving himself a break which turned out to be short-lived when the Sixties really started to swing!

COUNTRY LIVING

In October 1962, we'd left the built-up urban area where we'd lived for several years and re-located to a small market town in rural south Lincolnshire. My dad was appointed to a new job as the Public Health Inspector and Surveyor for the town. In my family history box I have a copy of his letter of appointment and it records that he was to be paid an annual salary of £1,180 and he was offered the tenancy of a council house for us to live in. He was offered 50% of the removal expenses (twenty two pounds) and an essential car user allowance of £54 per year and five pence per mile while on official duties. Also a gas cooker would be installed in the kitchen of the council house and a garage erected at the side of the property. The out-going Public Health Inspector left dad a lovely letter of welcome.

Dear Norman,

I am enclosing a sheet of my headed notepaper and perhaps you will amend it for your own use and return it so I can get an order off to the local printers in order that you may have the convenience of your own headed notepaper as soon as possible after commencing this appointment.

I will leave slaughter house keys and office keys with Miss B-- and I have arranged for a card of authority to be ready for you on the 22nd. The Clerk of the Council will no doubt introduce you to the office machinery and Miss B-- will explain the "chaos" of our filing system, records and administration but if at any time you feel that I can help you in any matter relating to your post please do not hesitate to contact me.

You seem to have made a very good impression on my young son for he has daily asked when next you are coming for lunch!

I do wish you all the very best in your new appointment and hope that you, your wife and family will settle very happily.

Yours sincerely,

Lionel.

How nice is that? The keys to the slaughter house, mentioned in the letter, were an important part of dad's job because it was his responsibility to ensure that no contaminated meat entered the food chain. He'd undertaken a special course in meat inspection a few years earlier. In his previous job he'd worked for part of the time in an industrial scale slaughter house. After we moved to Lincolnshire I went with him to the slaughter house on a couple of occasions. I was horrified at the stench and the blood splattered walls. The disgusting growths, ulcers and carbuncles on the contaminated meat had to be painted with a yellow dye, stamped with my dad's own, personal ID and declared unfit for human consumption. If I'd realised it was an option I would have become a vegetarian! However, meat and two veg was the staple of our mother's cooking, and meat and two veg was what we had for dinner. My dad's job also included organising pest control and managing the refuse collections. When the Council bought a replacement dustbin wagon it painted my dad's name on the side of the driver's cab and we teased him a lot about that.

At first we found our new part of the country a totally different planet. When living in Wakefield we were accustomed to visiting the countryside for outings but rarely spent more than a day there. Now we were surrounded by fields as far as the eye could see. There weren't many shops in the town; the buses ran occasionally rather than frequently; and the nearest larger towns of Stamford, Grantham, Lincoln and Peterborough were miles away. The town had been on the railway network until the Beeching axe closed both lines and the only remaining public transport was provided by a small family bus company. The company had been running a horse drawn bus service since 1890 but by the 1960s the firm were using double-deckers in a trademark blue and white livery.

Fortunately we'd had the luxury of a car for a couple of years: a second hand Ford Consul my parents had bought with the proceeds of a cancelled insurance policy. Soon after our move this was replaced by the Morris Minor with the dodgy gearstick. That car must have been jinxed. It didn't last long as it was involved in a head on collision with a speeding motorbike when my new, youngest sister was still a tiny baby. At the time of the accident my mother was in the front passenger seat with the baby on her lap. Amazingly, there were no serious injuries but both the motorbike and the car were write-offs. My mother's nerves were shattered and the incident justified all her anxieties about motoring.

My dad bought another Morris Minor but this was one of the "Traveller" design with the solid wood rear frame and double doors at the back. It was pale blue and the registration was YCT 840. That's not written down anywhere; I've always remembered it. When visiting the "Heartbeat" garage in Goathland (Aidensfield in the TV series) on the North Yorkshire moors I saw exactly the same model of Traveller but it had a different registration number. I was instantly transported back to my childhood and felt a warm glow of recognition.

To the north and west of the town the landscape was slightly hilly but to the south and east it was flat. Very flat. It wasn't long before I learned to ride a bike and was given a second hand Raleigh "Palm Springs". The bike became a necessity to get to my new school which was situated on the outskirts of the town more than a mile from where we were living. The bike had a black and white check saddle, Hawaiian scenes painted on the frame and a dynamo to make the lights work. Not that my sister and I went out at night very often. Usually we went for our bike rides in the school holidays or at weekends. With a few jam sandwiches and a bottle of orange squash in the saddle bags we were off for the day. We could easily cycle twenty miles along the long, straight fenland roads with a ditch on one side and views to the next village clearly in sight. Even though this was the era of the notorious Moors Murders, our parents had every confidence that we could go out for most of the day and return home safely before it was dark.

I started to attend the Grammar School and my younger sister went to the primary school. The uniform at the Grammar School was bottle green and the hats were "baker-boy" style. At the starting school interview the Headmaster said that as I'd just got a new navy blue school uniform a few weeks previously it would be okay to wear that until I grew out of it. Fortunately, my mum put her foot down and insisted I had a new, green outfit despite the extra expense. I was delighted she did. Like any new girl in a strange school I didn't want to be an object of curiosity any more than was necessary. The last thing I wanted was to stick out like a sore thumb in navy blue when everyone else was wearing bottle green!

The lessons were largely the same as Rothwell Grammar School although some of the teachers were more memorable. Especially Miss Fairbanks who was known to the whole school as "Flo". Miss Fairbanks was the formidable teacher of French who needed a walking stick to help her get about the school. She used her stick to good effect to thump on the front desks if she thought insufficient attention was being paid to her attempts to get us to sound like native French speakers with an exaggerated and over-pronounced rolling, expectorant "r". AHRRRR!

The school had the novel and enlightened idea that boys as well as girls would learn cooking and girls as well as boys would learn woodwork. In the third form we spent one half day for one whole term in a fully equipped kitchen somewhere off-site learning to cook. By the end of the course we knew how to make a cup of tea, a bowl of blancmange and a shepherd's pie. For woodwork we went to the school's workshop and learned how to hammer panel pins and cut corners out of bits of wood. We combined these useful skills to make a letter rack, although we were also allowed to use some wood glue to ensure the rack didn't fall apart on first usage.

The woodwork teacher was Mr Rayner. He was known as "Jackie" and was a man of very upright bearing. It was rumoured that he'd been injured during the War and wore a corset. This may or may not have been the case but in the harsh winter of 1962 - 1963, Mr Rayner proved to be a star. The school playing fields had become flooded and formed a small lake. This froze into solid ice and for several weeks the school had its own ice-rink for slipping and sliding. One lunchtime, Mr Rayner arrived at the ice-rink and changed into a pair of skates. He stepped out onto the ice and proceeded to demonstrate an extraordinary ability to turn figure-of-eights, skate on one leg with the other leg at right angles to his body and spin countless times without falling over. To say we were over-awed would be an understatement. We watched in silent appreciation until the end of his performance which was greeted with enthusiastic applause.

For the third term of the third year we had sewing with Mrs Foster, the Headmaster's wife. This was for girls only and I suppose the boys did some more demanding woodwork. Our sewing task was to make a soft toy. I thought it would be a great idea to make something for the baby. I chose the pattern of a toy swan and carefully traced it onto a piece of yellow felt. Left-handed scissors were not available, and so my cutting-out was erratic. After carefully sewing the pieces together with blanket stitch it became obvious that the swan's neck was too narrow to take much stuffing. No problem: I could use a piece of wire to push some stuffing into the neck and leave the wire in place to keep the neck upright. A couple of beads had already been sewn onto the swan's head for eyes. The toy was stuffed with Kapok, a light, water resistant and highly flammable fluff obtained from the seed pods of a tropical tree. I proudly took the yellow swan home for the baby and was perplexed when my mum decided it should take pride of place on a high shelf in the baby's bedroom, well out of reach.

Mr Foster, our Headmaster, was keen to get to know us all and in order to do so taught Latin to each form for one lesson each week. He also commanded the school in daily assembly and reached soaring heights of oratory at the annual Speech Day. On one such occasion in 1949, he'd achieved some considerable local notoriety with a speech in which he'd forcefully asserted the rights of teachers to be free from political interference in determining the curriculum. In his speech he complained of modern politicians who interfered not only with examinations but also with holidays and the freedoms of the grammar schools. He told his audience that the politicians would have "all of us, governors, staff and pupils alike, strung up like puppets. They have fallen in love with the power they have to jerk and dangle the strings and they have forgotten that at the other end there is flesh and blood." Afterwards at a meeting of the Kesteven County Council, Councillor Millet accused Mr Foster of "tub thumping" and repudiated his assertions. Councillor Millet had plenty more to say but the Chairman of the County Council, Alderman Sir Robert Pattinson, shut him up by ruling that it was improper for a head teacher to make any such comments and hoped that it would be understood that "we don't agree with that sort of thing!"

Mr Foster and the teachers wore their academic gowns routinely every day but added their colourful hoods and a sprinkling of mortar boards for Speech Day. The Chair of Governors was Mrs Nesta Trollope-Bellew and she presented me with a Speech Day prize at the start of the third year. The prize was the second volume of Mozart Piano Sonatas. A special label was glued inside the front cover to say it was presented to me for making good progress in the previous year and it was signed by Nesta Trollope-Bellew.

Mrs Trollope-Bellew joined the school governing body in 1933. She was a direct descendent of a benefactor of the school, William Trollope, who re-built the old school building in 1626. At his death ten years later, William Trollope left an endowment of £30 per year to pay the teacher's salary. Nesta was the oldest child of Major Hon. Robert Cranmer Trollope (who appears to be from a different lineage to the famous novelist) and his wife Ethel Mary Carew. In 1901, when Nesta was about twelve years old, the family lived at Crowcombe Court House in Somerset. The beautiful house was built by Thomas Carew, designed by Nathaniel Ireson and completed in 1739. It stayed in the Carew family until the mid twentieth century and is now a wedding and corporate hospitality venue. Nesta's father was the local Magistrate who "lived on his own means". These means were sufficient to employ a French governess for Nesta. In addition to Mlle Appolina Periel, Major Trollope employed a cook, a lady's maid, two laundry maids, a kitchen maid, a schoolroom maid, a housemaid, a footman and a butler.

Nesta's father died in 1908 and her mother went to live with her own widowed mother in South Kensington. The fifteen roomed house was in a good location just off the Cromwell Road. To look after them the two ladies had a butler, a housekeeper, a footman, two housemaids, a kitchen maid and their own personal lady's maid. Nesta, however, stayed on at the forty four roomed Crowcombe Court with her friend, the twenty year old Nancy Burrows-Hill and the eight servants who were looking after them! At the end of 1911, Nesta sailed on the P&O steamship "Malloja" to Bombay, India, in the company of the Lord Londesborough, the Hon. Sybil Fellowes, Lady Irene Dennison, Lord Leigh and the Duke of Hamilton to attend the imperial coronation of George V and Queen Alexandra at the Delhi Durbar.

Nesta married Lt. Colonel Froude Dillon Bellew in 1918. The Lt. Colonel had his name changed to Trollope by Royal Licence in 1920 and Nesta became known as the Hon. Mrs Trollope-Bellew. When I shook her hand at the Speech Day in 1964 Mrs Trollope-Bellew was seventy five years old and seemed to me to be a very ancient and formidable lady indeed. I felt a curtsey would be in order. She died in 1975 and a memorial stone was erected in her ancestral home at Crowcombe.

I suppose I was given a book of music for the prize because I'd taken to doing piano practice, together with another pupil, on the school's Steinway grand in the school hall. Occasionally, we accompanied the assembly hymns. I'd started going to a new piano teacher in Stamford who was far more business-like than the inspirational Miss Heaps who'd been my first piano teacher. The weekly trips to Stamford for piano lessons were greatly enjoyed by my dad who was in seventh heaven with five parish churches to explore and streets of houses straight out of a Jane Austen novel.

Although my new piano teacher was much more strict and austere than the lovely Miss Heaps, she was very keen on getting her pupils to perform in the local music festival competitions. She matched her pupils into pairs to enter the piano duet competitions and she found me a partner who lived locally. This girl quickly became a friend and I loved going to her house for tea and piano practice. Her parents ran a residential home for children and at any time there would be a dozen or more children of all ages living there. The atmosphere was warm and lively and tea ended with unlimited slices of bread and jam. After tea, on sunny afternoons, we all went out to play in the garden before starting our piano practice. We didn't win the duet competition but the preparation was great fun.

Moving to a small country town meant several other adjustments. Instead of a large, purpose-built, municipal library, the public library was just one room in a converted house that was also used for civic offices. The children's library was only a couple of shelves in a corner of the adult library: a complete contrast to the library we'd used previously in Wakefield. However, the school library was substantial so there was no shortage of reading material in our new location. Anyway, in our new public library thirteen year olds could transfer to the adult shelves and as the stock was renewed regularly there was always plenty of choice. It wasn't long before I discovered Georgette Heyer, Jean Plaidy and Anya Seaton. Ah, the pleasure of historical romances!

We were accustomed to going shopping in big northern cities where there were large shops that you could spend ages nosing around. Now all the shops were small, mainly for groceries and hardware. You were expected to just go in, buy what you needed and leave. There was little scope for browsing. Except in the shop which sold fabric and everything needed for dressmaking including patterns. Our mum had made our clothes herself since we were small. As we got older we liked to go with her to the fabric shop and choose our own designs and patterns. When we were young she'd economised by making two of each outfit and my younger sister and I were dressed the same as though we were twins. As we got older our tastes diverged and we made our own choices. My favourite dress was a Simplicity pattern with puff sleeves, a button front and a centre pleat. The fabric I chose had a version of the iconic sixties Mary Quant daisy printed on it in pastel shades and it had a matching draw string bag. But the days of home-made clothes were coming to an end as the lure of boutiques increased.

Some Saturdays we visited Lincoln or Peterborough. Although there weren't as many department stores as in Leeds, at least there were Woolworths, Boots and British Home Stores. We would visit the Cathedral in each town to admire the architecture and on the journey my dad, as usual, would make a diversion to visit some small country parish church.

Every few months we went back to Yorkshire to visit our relatives. This was quite a trek as the A1, or Great North Road as it was known, hadn't yet been turned into dual carriageway. For many miles it was a dangerous three lane road with drivers in each direction vying for the overtaking lane.

However, the biggest adjustment we had to make in our new life was nothing to do with the town. At the end of 1963 we had acquired a new baby sister. Although there was a gooseberry bush in the large garden of our rented council house, the baby wasn't found under it but in the maternity ward of Peterborough General Hospital. I was a Yorkshire Tyke; my younger sister was a Derbyshire Tup; and now we had a Lincolnshire Yellow-Belly in the family. Always a reminder to our father of his pursuit of promotion across three counties of England.

When we went to collect my mum and the new baby from the hospital we were transfixed by the tiny, doll-like form. She was fast asleep but on arriving home we took turns in holding her so it wasn't long before she woke up. She was swaddled in a pretty, lacy shawl. As she opened her eyes, her face turned red, she took a deep breath and she let out the loudest, piercing scream I had ever heard in my life. It was incredible that such a tiny baby could have such a massive pair of lungs. These were used to great effect over the next two years to let us know when she was displeased one way or another.

This was the age of washable nappies. We had an electric boiler which stood in the corner of the kitchen emitting steam all day, every day, to ensure a constant supply of pristine white squares of cotton. The nappies were hung like bunting on the washing line to dry off whenever it stopped raining. Otherwise they were suspended over the rungs of a clothes horse and then even more steam condensed on the iron framed windows and puddled onto the floor beneath.

The baby had a four wheeled, well sprung carriage in which to be pushed out every day for some health giving fresh air. The fashion, prevalent in the fifties, for parking the baby out in the garden whatever the weather for several hours had passed and a brisk walk every day was all that was required. After a few months we moved into a new house. Finally, our parents had managed to save enough money for a deposit and negotiated a mortgage. The house had central heating and big picture windows which made it light and airy. It was right on the western edge of the town overlooking open fields so sufficiently far enough away from the town centre to rock the baby to sleep before reaching the shops.

Despite the considerable contrast, we gradually became accustomed to our new home and began to enjoy living there. I joined the Girl Guides where the sub-groups were called patrols and named after flowers. I was in the Primroses at first and later the Daffodils. We met every week in an old hut and continued to explore the joys of nature and community service. We sang carols to elderly folk at Christmas; hymns to patients in the cottage hospital on special occasions; and paraded through the town with other uniformed groups, young and old, at Armistice and civic events.

There was also a youth club to join which I did as soon as I was thirteen, the minimum age for enrolment. Soon Friday nights were for pop records, dancing and giggling. Occasionally, we were entertained by the town's very own boy band, "The Maniax". After they released a record in 1966 the band's reputation locally was secure. "Out of Reach" with "The Devil's Home" on the B side didn't get into the charts but as far as we were concerned it was a Number One Hit and we all gave it "foive". The band comprised Ian on drums and his brother Alan playing the Hammond Organ; Peter was the bass guitar and Johnnie played lead guitar; while the singer was Mick. "Out of Reach" was sold locally along with autographed photo postcards of the group and we were in seventh heaven with our very own band to swoon over. The band toured as a supporting act to several better known groups before a stint in Germany and their eventual break-up. My copy of "Out of Reach" and my autographed photo has survived countless house re-locations and is currently somewhere in my youngest sister's loft waiting for its turn on the Antiques Roadshow. "Out of Reach" was written by Mikis Theodorakis of Zorba the Greek fame. Another Maniax fan has put the B side "The Devil's Home" on YouTube. A comment-writer notes that they'd seen the band at a local agricultural show and asks if the band originated in the area. Someone else (webbywoo) confirms that they were local and that the singer was his grandad.

Sunday nights were for the church youth group with attendance at Evensong and Confirmation classes expected but many opted out of the latter. A couple of years later I joined the Anglican Young People's Association which had the same weekly offering as the youth club but the added bonus of attending the annual rally of the AYPA in some distant location. The year I went it was Bournemouth and in addition to talks and discussion groups there were beach barbeques and swimming in the sea. Overnight accommodation was offered by local

51

people who must have been dragooned by their local vicar into offering bed and breakfast to unknown teenagers. Our parents didn't know who we were staying with so there was a huge amount of trust on all sides for the event to take place. But it did, and we had lots of fun.

Before our family re-located to the Lincolnshire countryside we used to go regularly to the Halle Orchestra concerts in Leeds and Bradford. These were now sorely missed by my father as there wasn't anything similar in our new rural location. So, in the summer of 1965 my dad decided we would go to London to the BBC Proms at the Royal Albert Hall. We'd been to London for a short holiday a few years earlier but the excitement of London, especially now it was Swinging, was even greater than before. We had a day ticket and caught the train from Peterborough railway station on August 19th and were in the capital a couple of hours later. My dad decided that our education would benefit from an immersion in art and we spent much of the day in the National Gallery. The highlight of the visit was seeing the Leonardo Cartoon which had been purchased a couple of years earlier by the gallery after a well-publicised appeal for donations. A brisk walk round St James' Park and a Lyons Corner House for something to eat and then we headed to South Kensington for the concert.

We were not only overawed by the vastness of the Albert Hall but also by the size of the audience which was far greater than anything we'd experienced before. The programme started with Neville Marriner directing the Academy of St Martin in the Fields in a Handel concerto while he played the violin. Impressive! This was followed by the premiere of Michael Tippett's piano concerto conducted by the composer himself. The soloist was John Ogden and the music was execrable. After the interval Malcolm Sargent conducted the BBC Symphony Orchestra and the BBC Singers in a performance of "The Planets". We'd been listening to this on a gramophone record for weeks and loved every minute. Unfortunately, we couldn't stay long for the applause at the end as we had to get back to King's Cross to catch the train home. It was a wonderful day out and sowed the seed that I really must go and live in London when I was older.

The summer of 1965 was the high spot of my Girl Guiding career when some of our Guide troop had the opportunity to go on a two week camping trip in Wales. I bought an enamel plate and mug plus a set of camping cutlery and hired a sleeping bag from the Girl Guides' communal store. As the sleeping bags weren't laundered between hirings I also borrowed a cotton sheet liner to put inside it. When the trip was over the liner had to be washed at home before returning it to the store. I packed all my kit into a big, heavy rucksack that my dad had brought back from the War and set off on a coach which went all round the Lincolnshire countryside picking up the other happy campers.

We'd practised for the trip by learning how to cook outdoors in a biscuit tin. We went to the woods on the edge of town with one of those twelve inch cube shaped Fox's biscuits tins in which we normally stored our first aid kit. The idea was to use the tin as an oven and build a small fire inside it. When the fire was reduced to glowing embers we intended to cook sausages skewered on a long stick. Naturally, it didn't work and we were left with a filthy tin and a couple of raw sausages. I threw my sausage away but my friend ate hers. Miraculously, she was still able to come to Wales.

On arrival at the camp site the bell tents were already pitched. They were clearly the same ones used by Baden Powell at Mafeking. The side sections had to be rolled up each morning to let some air into the tent. Each tent accommodated about a dozen girls plus several million earwigs and daddy longlegs. We had a smelly, rubber ground sheet on which to place the sleeping bag and a good night's sleep was determined by the presence, or not, of stones in the grass, rather like the princess and the pea. In the morning, once the sleeping bags had been aired in the sun (or wind, or rain) they were rolled up and stored on the bedding racks. We made these frames out of branches lashed together at the corners with string. Not surprisingly, the bedding racks often collapsed and needed frequent repair.

The mornings were spent in chores around the campsite with each group of girls taking turns in cooking patrol, washing-up patrol, litter patrol and latrine patrol. Unbelievably, the latter actually involved pairs of girls carrying the buckets from beneath the chemical toilets to a pit dug in the next field into which each smelly bucket was emptied. However, the job didn't take long and when on latrine patrol the rest of the morning could be spent in "free time". There was a stream running along one edge of the camp site and we soon realised that on the other side of it, a couple of fields further along, was a similar camp site for Boy Scouts. They were all from Hemel Hempstead which was some unknown place down south but they were friendly enough and latrine patrol soon became the best chore on the rota.

In the afternoons we went on outings to places of interest in the area and visited Abergavenny, Llangorse Lake, Tretower Court, Crickhowell and Brecon Cathedral. In the evenings a camp fire was lit and we sat round it in the dusk listening to ghost stories, singing camp fire songs and being eaten to death by midges. Unfortunately, the last couple of days of the camp were marred when the meat for the stew, which was kept in a meat safe in the trees, went off and the whole camp was beset by upset stomachs. Lots of absentees on latrine duty that day. Nevertheless, as intrepid Girl Guides we were not defeated and returned home asserting that the trip to Wales had been the best holiday of our lives thus far!

POUNDS, SHILLINGS AND PENCE

I stayed in the Girl Guides until I was fifteen and continued to undertake the Willing Shilling fund-raising week every year. Some of the jobs resulted in offers of further work when Willing Shilling was over. A couple of the car owners commissioned me to return to give their car the once-over. Autumn leaf sweeping in a few of the bigger houses, surrounded by massive chestnut trees, added more than a few shillings to my coffers. This do-jobs-to-earn-money ethic learned at Brownies and Girl Guides resonated with my upbringing and I put it into practice throughout adolescence.

A year after moving to Lincolnshire, we heard about an exciting opportunity to increase the supply of readies. We were tipped off by a couple of our new friends to go, after school, to a certain street on the edge of the town, hide our bikes behind the hedge and wait. A lorry would come and take the assembled school kids far out into the surrounding countryside and deposit us in the pea fields. To do this we had to dash home quickly from school, change into some scruffy clothes, grab some bread and jam and get back to the assembly point before the lorry passed through. It was an open truck with low sides and we scrambled onto it and clung to each other as it hurtled along. Fortunately, the roads were long and straight and no-one ever flew off.

On arrival at the pea fields we gave our names to the teller and collected boxes which we had to fill with pea pods. Each time the box was filled it was taken back to the teller's table, weighed and the amount entered against our names. We picked the peas as fast as we could but were far out-paced by the travelling people and their families who made up the remainder of the work force. As dusk started to fall, work stopped and everyone lined up at the teller's table to be paid in cash for the weight of peas picked. Then, as no-one wanted to be left behind and stuck in the middle of nowhere, it was a mad dash for the transport and another knuckle-clenching ride back to the pick-up point.

Having re-assured ourselves the bikes were still behind the hedge where we'd left them, we all went to the chippy for battered sausages and chips paid for with some of the proceeds of our efforts. The season was short and during the day gangs of adult workers went to the fields so we never returned to the same spot twice. By the end of the pea harvest we were several pounds better off although our homework suffered and our clothes became permeated with the nauseating odour of peas.

Newspaper rounds were coveted and children were supposed to be thirteen before taking one on. However, the rules for a Sunday paper round were more lax. I had a friend who'd got a Sunday paper round but didn't want to do it every week. Several weeks before my thirteenth birthday I started helping out and eventually took over the job. The round came with its own handcart made from a wooden packing case affixed to a set of pram wheels that was pulled along by a rope handle. The papers were collected at the newsagent's and loaded into the cart and delivered early on Sunday morning in time for the customers to read with their bacon, eggs and fried bread. This part of the job was completed by about ten o'clock. The next few hours were free until mid-afternoon when it was time to go round again and collect the money. This was a very hit and miss affair and it was essential to keep accurate records each week of who had paid and who had not. In addition to paying for their papers the customers had to pay a delivery charge as well. At the end of each Sunday afternoon the round book had to be totted up and the money that was due to the newsagent handed over. The delivery charge was kept by me along with any tips that kindly customers had bestowed. Not everyone paid up willingly and occasionally arguments occurred about what had been paid, to whom and when. Hence the need to keep the round book completely up-to-date. After four weeks, customers who declined to pay were advised by the newsagent that their order wouldn't be fulfilled any more. In a small town this rule was easily imposed so it didn't happen very often but a few customers did push it to the limit. The newsagent expected the newspaper boy (or in my case, girl) to make all efforts to get paid and didn't deal kindly with any excuses. All in all it was very character forming! But most people were nice, tips were good and the job was well worth doing.

When I was fifteen we moved house yet again as my dad got another promotion and we re-located back to Yorkshire. Some young people might have resented the constant upheaval occasioned by my father's promotions but I certainly didn't. I found it exciting to move to new places, meet new people and face new challenges. I think it had a positive effect upon my character. It made me resilient, flexible and willing to embrace innovations and change.

On the downside, our latest re-location meant that the lucrative leaf sweeping, pea-pulling and newspaper round came to an end. I left the Girl Guides and didn't re-enrol but the need to get my hands on more money to fund my teenage life-style continued to increase. Records, makeup, clothes, magazines and Saturday night dances required a steady flow of cash far in excess of my weekly pocket money.

I was an experienced and proficient baby-sitter and after we'd moved it wasn't long before I found an easy way to supplement my income. I did a few initial baby-sitting jobs for the children of teachers at school and then landed the dream baby-sitting job. A new luxury housing estate, with architect designed houses reflecting all the attributes of Sixties taste and style, had been built on the edge of the town. Mr and Mrs Brown were affluent, youngish parents in their mid-thirties who commuted to work in Leeds. Once each week they went locally, after work, to play badminton tournaments. My job was to arrive just after the two children, aged six and eight, had been given tea by their mum. I had to play with the children for an hour or so and then send them to bed and read them a bedtime story. After making sure they went to sleep I looked after them until their parents arrived home at about ten thirty.

The children were as good as gold and went off to sleep straight away. This left me with plenty of time to do my homework and watch TV. The Browns had a big, colour TV which was still a novelty then so I really enjoyed that. They also had a parquet floor in dark wood blocks with a rug woven in bright exotic colours positioned in the middle of the room. There was a baby grand piano and floor to ceiling French doors that opened straight into the back garden. To complete this vision of total, trendy Sixties chic the Browns had a large open stone dish on a side table containing several terrapins under a spotlight. The kitchen and dining area were open plan and I was told to help myself to coffee and biscuits. (Nescafe Blend 37 and Jacobs' Club.) The Browns' cups and saucers were chunky Wedgewood in dark blue and they even had a dish washer. They paid 7/6 and extra if I went for occasional Saturday nights.

Despite the regular baby-sitting, I still didn't have enough cash and decided I needed a Saturday job. Woolies was my preferred employer as there was a branch in the High Street. It seemed like half the girls in my year at school were after a job there; or at the fruit and veg shop or the pork butchers. My applications were turned down so I had to cast my net wider and write off to the managers of Boots the Chemist and W.H. Smiths in York. My aim was the record department in the basement at WHS but the manager decided I was better suited to the toy department. For over a year I caught the early morning Saturday train, donned my blue nylon overall, fixed a smile on my face and prepared to help the under tens part with their pocket money and birthday money. Believe me, this was no picnic. Not all the children were as well behaved as those I encountered when baby-sitting. Some of the junior customers had no concept of retail and seemed to think the WHS toy department was a permanent Santa's grotto. At the end of the day it was time to line up at the manager's office and collect the pay: 18/6 in cash in a little brown envelope always made such challenging days worthwhile.

Chelsea Girl had opened a branch almost next door to WHS and I often spent my lunch break in there deciding what I could afford to buy for my Saturday night-out. As soon as I was let out of WHS I dashed back into Chelsea Girl to buy whatever had caught my eye. One week it was a mini-kilt which was so short my dad went apoplectic when I appeared in it. Most of all, though, I wanted something from Biba which had opened its first store in Kensington in 1964. I kept seeing stories in teen magazines about Biba and in 1969 they put out a catalogue for mail order. I never managed to order anything from the catalogue: the prices were too high for my measly wages!

When our A Levels were over, my friend and I got summer holiday jobs as waitresses in a large hotel on the Essex coast. It was an awfully big adventure! Our head teacher didn't want us to leave school until the end of term and she gave us a stern talking to. My parents were none too enthusiastic about the plan either and put up as many obstacles as they could think of. But nothing would put us off and we caught a train to London and navigated our way on the Underground to Liverpool Street station. There we caught another train to take us on to the seaside and the hotel.

We lived in a staff house behind the hotel for three months. My friend and I shared the same room. Each bedroom in the staff house was sub-divided by a plywood partition to create cubicles surrounding just a bed and a chest of drawers. The "wardrobe" was a couple of hooks in the wall on which to hang our clothes! The wallpaper was old; the paintwork was scuffed; and the curtains were drab, dusty and insecurely attached to the curtain rail. It was a bit of a shock after my lovely bedroom at home in Yorkshire.

We had to provide our own uniforms and, even though she strongly disapproved of me going to work in the hotel, my mum made me a little black skirt to wear with my white school blouses. This was just about acceptable to the manageress of the hotel restaurant. She told us we would have to purchase a little white, frilly, nylon apron from a catering shop to complete the look. The apron was washed out daily in the hand basin in the staff house and drip-dried overnight.

We earned about seven pounds a week in addition to our accommodation and food. We could also keep any tips we received. We worked shifts and had one and half days off each week. Between shifts we were free to go where we pleased but there wasn't much that could be fitted in between the end of breakfast at ten thirty and the start of lunch at twelve. Lunch finished at two thirty and then dinner commenced at five thirty and went on until the last diner left the restaurant. With such a busy timetable the day off became greatly treasured.

Our day off wasn't fixed but changed every week to ensure that on any day only one waitress was off. Occasionally on our day off it was necessary to cover for another member of staff who was sick. This meant our own day off was lost and forgotten by the management. For the first few weeks on my days off I mooched around the town and enjoyed visiting the shops, the beach, the pier and the amusements. This eventually palled and I began to look for alternatives. I located the bus station and checked out the timetable. I found that there were several service buses to other towns in the area and I spent a few of my days off visiting them. I loved Roman Colchester and went there twice. But we rarely forgot we were at the hotel to earn money to take to college and so spending it on treats and outings was kept to a minimum.

The hotel had a bizarre method of accounting: the cash register kept a record of all food ordered by customers against the name of each waitress. At the end of the shift the cash register printed out a summary of the meals served by each waitress and their overall cost. However, we each had to hang on to the money we collected from the customers and keep it in a purse, along with the tips, until the end of the shift. While we were working the tables the purses were kept next to the cash register. When the shift finished we had to give the correct amount of money printed on the summary to the manageress. If there was any shortfall this had to be made up by the waitress out of her own money. On one shift all my takings mysteriously disappeared out of my purse so I had to pay for all the dinners eaten by the customers out of my own previously hard-earned cash. As this happened during the week, it wasn't a huge amount. Thank heavens it didn't happen on Saturday night when the restaurant was always full.

When they'd finished their meal, most customers usually gave the waitress a tip of a shilling or two. One day there was a single penny under the table mat of each of four diners to whom I'd served a three course meal. This didn't impress me very much but this, I'm glad to say, was the exception. If customers complained about the food it was taken back to the kitchen where it was re-arranged on the plate by the assistant chef; ceremonially spat over and then returned to the restaurant. Which is why whenever I dine out I never send anything back no matter how foul it tastes and I always tip the server generously.

When the hotel was short staffed we had to help out as chambermaids. The back stairs went from the kitchen area into the main hotel. There was often a beetle or two on the stairs and I became adept at avoiding them. I'm not sure if they were cockroaches but they seemed to live there permanently. There were no baths in the staff house and so a bathroom in the hotel was designated for staff use. The beetles lived in the bathroom too and I went there as little as possible.

There was a small TV in the staff lounge and on 21st July we watched in awe as images from the moon were transmitted into our lives. However, we didn't linger. The moon was a long way off and customers needed serving. I celebrated my eighteenth birthday at the hotel. For my birthday present, my mum sent me a leather writing case equipped with notepaper, envelopes, a fountain pen and six stamps!

Towards the end of August, the waiter who served the drinks at the evening meals left the job and I asked the manageress if I could take over. Although the tips were minimal, this job was a big improvement because all the drinks the customers wanted in the restaurant had to be brought from the bar in the hotel. The bar was adjacent to the room where the hotel Disco was held and while waiting for the drinks to be served I could enjoy whatever records were being played that night. On Friday and Saturday nights there was live music too. I quickly acquired the knack of carrying several pint pots of beer in one hand leaving the other hand free for opening the doors; a useful skill for later life I've found. I struggled to learn how to get a tray of drinks to the table without some spillage until I stopped looking at the tray and then miraculously it seemed to balance. Once a group of guests ordered a bottle of celebratory Asti Spumante to be served at their table. The bar manager told me to remove the wrappings and just flick the cork off the top. He omitted any warnings about shaking the bottle so when I pushed the top off, the cork shot out of the bottle at considerable speed. It flew across the restaurant, narrowly missing a baby in a high chair and landed on the table at the other end of the room. Fortunately no-one was sitting there and the good natured audience gave me a round of applause.

At the end of the season we packed our bags and made the journey back to Yorkshire. We'd saved over a hundred pounds and were satisfied that our hard work had been worthwhile. It had been exciting travelling via London. Now I was looking forward even more to going there to start college.

The following year, during our college vacations, my sister and I found holiday jobs in a bacon factory. Despite the neck-to-knee, thick cotton overall and 1940s style turban, we were not protected from the smell. By the end of the shift we were impregnated with it, especially if it had been a smoky bacon day. We biked home as fast as we could and raced each other to the shower but even so the smell lingered. Clocking on was at eight in the morning and we clocked off at four in the afternoon. The work was tedious and tiring but highly lucrative as basic pay was eighteen pounds a week plus overtime and students didn't pay income tax.

My job was to stand beside a conveyor belt and lift, without gloves, three pound catering portions of pre-weighed, glutinous, pre-sliced bacon from the belt and slide it into a plastic wrapper. The bacon slices were then returned to the conveyor belt and the next lump of passing dead pig was grabbed. Sometimes something would go wrong at the end of the conveyor belt and it would become congested by the quantity of packs of bacon waiting to be moved off for distribution. But the three pound lumps kept on coming towards us regardless and had to be stacked up and stacked up until it occurred to one of the technicians to turn the conveyor belt off. It was very noisy in the factory and the regulars were proficient in lip-reading. We students who did not possess this skill were effectively rendered speechless and passed the day listening to the pop records played non-stop at full volume which managed to swamp even the noise of the machinery.

Toilet breaks were strictly organised by the "blue-top" in charge of the line. These formidable women, identified by the blue turbans they all wore, told us when to go to the toilet. Even if we didn't need to go, it was necessary to take a turn because this was really a fag-break, compulsory even for those who didn't smoke. Not compulsory according to the management, of course, but compulsory according to the blue-tops. Management organised the operation with buzzers at the start and end of shifts and official tea and dinner breaks, but it was the blue-tops who were effectively running the factory.

To get to the toilets for the fag-break it was necessary to pass through the department that dealt with condemned meat. Here, the pig carcasses were rendered down for pet food. In this department the stench was even worse although the noise was less. This meant that the ribald commentary prompted by the appearance of every woman passing through the section was easily heard. The air was blue even though faces might be red. However, the pay packets at the bacon factory compensated for everything and by the end of the summer both my sister and I had healthy bank balances.

The final casual job I had was as a tea-lady in the offices of a national charity. I'd gone to an employment agency who for my first job sent me to a GPO telephone exchange where an assistant breakfast cook was desperately needed to cover a sickness absence. At the time I thought I was an odd choice for this assignment as I had no mass catering experience - in fact, I could barely cook. However I needed a job and so, wasn't going to argue. The telephone engineers were accustomed to getting a full fry-up with unlimited slices of fried bread and cups of tea. The cook-in-charge took one look at me, screamed with rage at my lack of experience, total incompetence and complete failure to crack an egg without splitting the yolk and gave me my marching orders. In floods of tears I returned to the employment agency where Elizabeth, the owner, apologised to me and said she'd been obliged by her contract to send someone, anyone, and I was the sacrifice.

However, as a reward for my valiant efforts, Elizabeth now had the perfect job for me. I was to go to the headquarters of a national charity where full training would be given for the role of tea-lady. The regular tea-lady had broken her arm and quit the job. The full training took about ten minutes. The job consisted of boiling some kettles, filling up a tea urn with hot water and loading a trolley with cups and saucers. The tea trolley was wheeled alongside the desks of the army of staff employed to open envelopes and process the cash and cheques sent in as donations to the charity. After handing out the teas all that was required was to go round again later, collect up the pots, do the washing up and repeat the whole process in the afternoon. In addition, I had to provide a tray service for the secretaries on the mezzanine floor who were all Sloane Rangers and looked as though they'd stepped straight off the pages of Vogue.

In the afternoons, if any of the directors of the charity had come in they had china tea cups and cakes but that didn't happen very often. Even so, on the off chance one of the directors would be in attendance a cook was employed to prepare lunch for them. The same kitchen which I used for the teas was fully fitted out for small scale catering. Often the request for lunch came at the last minute so the cook spent most of her time preparing food that could be brought from the fridge and cooked quickly. Most days she cooked lunch for herself and me too. I particularly enjoyed the grilled trout in Madeira sauce which was the cook's signature dish.

I enjoyed working as a tea-lady and made such a good impression on the charity's Personnel Officer that she offered me the job permanently.

No thanks!

No more Willing Shillings!

I'd had enough!

There was an expansion in higher education and a shortage of teachers for the children of the baby boomers. I'd been to a teacher training college, qualified as a primary teacher and was on the cusp of some of the best experiences of my life. But that's for another day!

AU REVOIR

Thank you for reading Jam for Tea. I hope you've enjoyed sharing my reminiscences and anecdotes; and I hope that I've prompted some memories of your own too.

Many thanks also to:

my husband, Michael Murray, for helping me write my books;

my sisters, Helen and Susan, for being part of my memories;
and my brother-in-law, Colin, for obtaining my copy of the British Trades Alphabet from Ebay.

I hope you'll want to read some more of our books.

They're all available from the Amazon website.

I Think I Prefer the Tinned Variety
The Diary of a Petty Officer in the Fleet Air Arm during World War II
N. Buckle & C. Murray

Seventy years ago, World War II uprooted my father, Norman Buckle, from a coal mining village in South Yorkshire and transported him thousands of miles to Sierra Leone in West Africa and later to a tropical island in the Pacific. "I Think I Prefer the Tinned Variety" presents the diary extracts Norman wrote when stationed at naval shore-bases in Freetown, Sierra Leone; Sidney, Australia; and Ponam in the Admiralty Islands. My own fascination with family history has lead me to research the background to the diary which is included as annotations to the text. The book is not an account of battles and action: it describes some of Norman's experiences far away from home and his everyday life as a shore-based radio mechanic during WW2.

A Single To Filey
Michael Murray

Detective Chief Inspector Tony Forward's hobby is directing amateur theatricals.

His latest production for the Sandleton-on-Sea Players is "The Cherry Orchard".

It's nearly midnight and he still hasn't completed the dress rehearsal. Then duty calls: a man with fatal head injuries has been discovered in a remote bay on the East Yorkshire coast.

The man's name is Mark Coulson and he's the Headteacher of a local primary school. But no-one seems able to explain why this respectable, professional man was at such an isolated spot so late at night. His wife is the most mystified of all.

Why were Mr Coulson's pockets empty? Sergeant Wilmott believes robbery was the motive. But if the killer had stolen Coulson's car keys why is his car still parked nearby?

Was Mr Coulson murdered by a jealous boyfriend or husband? That's what DC Diane Griffiths thinks. But Mr Coulson's Chair of Governors says he was a boring man whose only interest was his work.

With such a baffling case to solve how can DCI Forward find time for "The Cherry Orchard"?

All titles available from the Amazon website.

And finally: ... Odhu/ntinggo = good hunting!

Printed in Poland
by Amazon Fulfillment
Poland Sp. z o.o., Wrocław